EMPATH

A New Way to Understand Traits, Signs and The Dark Side to Being an Empath. Overcome Anxiety in Relationship and Build Mental Health.

Richard Kim

This report is intended to include precise and solid details on the protected point and problem. Output was made accessible with the expectation that the manufacturer would not be needed to have payroll, officially approved, or otherwise eligible administrations. In the event that the exhortation is relevant, lawful, or qualified, a person who has been rehearsed in a call will be required. The Statement of Standards approved and endorsed by the American Bar Association Committee and the Publications and Associations Commission.

The data given herein is articulated, to be truthful and consistent, in that any danger, in so far as absenteeism or otherwise, by the usage or misuse of any of the methods, procedures, or bearings found therein is a single and articulate responsibility of the beneficiary peruser. Through no way will any legal duty or liability be put on the seller for any reparation, loss or catastrophe relating to money on the grounds of the data stored therein, either explicitly or by inference. Different authors assert all copyrights not owned by the manufacturer. The data in this segment is given for educational purposes only and, as such, is all-inclusive, the details shall be entered into without a contract or other guarantee of security.

The markings used shall be without permission, and the delivery of the label shall be without the approval or help of the creator of the symbol. All logos and logos in this book are for clarification only and are specifically owned by the individuals who are not affiliated with this document.

Table of Contents

INTRODUCTION

Actually, being empathy itself is not a problem. When empathy for someone becomes firm and strong, that is problematic. When someone expresses what may look and even feel like empathy, but the underlying intention is manipulative, this can be a problem as well.

Empathy is considered an important component in a healthy relationship and it is for good reason.

Empathy is the capacity to be aware of and be sensitive to the feelings and emotions of others, and to feel part of what other experiences without being told exactly what is going on with him or her.

Whether we are going through a rough patch or a crisis, it is most always helpful to know how others care and share in our sorrow or pain.

However, misplaced and pseudo-empathy rarely are helpful, and can be harmful.

Did you know that empathy is not as natural for some people as you would expect it to be?
Empathy is a feeling of compassion for your fellow-man, anything or anyone on this planet of ours.

It is our responsibilities to engage others with empathy, and to show love and kindness to everyone around us. Understanding the power of empath opens so many doors for you and for me and for others in the same category.

Empathy is a global and noble calling that enables understanding, helpful acts of kindness or sheer comfort to an otherwise uncomfortable life, circumstance, or haunting situation.

It is apparent to make seeking or expressing empathy more of an action, without expectation, show empathy to the hurt, downtrodden or even to the most undeserving of human beings.

It's okay to feel and act upon empathy. Empathy is quite a better skill to demonstrate than covetousness, fear, judgement or jealousy. It brings understanding and help resolve different opinions or even produce more patience when presented with impractical situations.

Sometimes we get focused into situation for reasons that have no count. The best thing is to show yourself empathy, even if nobody else will. Quiet your mind, even when someone or a group of people are denying that they are causing you anguish or discomfort.

They are being covetous over your work, spoken words or your ability to acquire a skill that they themselves have not even tried to achieve for themselves.

If they would at least try, they would understand that acquiring a skill takes time and effort and cannot be regained and should not be repackaged. Turn that negative energy's direction around, toss it upside down!

This is a time to begin anew! Make this agonizing time ripe for resolution and solutions by planning in appropriate ways. Realizing what is happening, there is need to revisit your thoughts and align them with your mind, as this is the best time to focus on another avenue.

This book was born with the idea of understanding what an empathetic person is, understanding their discomfort in today's society and making efforts to fight to overcome them.

I have put a lot of effort into this first book on empathy, others will follow, and I hope you appreciate my efforts, for now, I thank you for your purchase and I hope for a positive review from you.

TRAITS OF AN EMPATH

Empaths are exceptionally receptive to others' temperaments, feelings and opinion. They feel everything, in some cases to an extraordinary.

They take on cynicism, for example, outrage or tension, which can cause a loss of energy for them. In the scenario that they are happy and feel loved, however, their bodies take these on and prosper.

The brand name of an empath is that they feel and ingest others' feelings and additional manifestations of emotions on account of their high sensitivities.

They channel the world through their instinct and struggle, intellectualizing their sentiments.

Empaths are normally giving, profoundly open, and great listeners. Empaths become overpowered in groups, which can intensify their compassion.

Empaths experience the world through their instinct. It is significant for them to build up their instinct and tune in to their premonitions about individuals.
This helps empaths discover positive connections and maintain a strategic distance from energy-depriving vampires.

Empaths are large hearted individuals and attempt to diminish the agony of others.

Thinking often about the emotions of others is something but extremely awful, however anxiety for another's challenges can eclipse your consideration for yourself.

This can factor into empathy weariness and burnout, so it's important to reserve some energy for yourself.

Empaths may likewise be more powerless against control or harmful practices. Your sincere response to help individuals in trouble can leave you ignorant of indications of danger.

It tends to be hard for empaths to shield themselves from taking on others' feelings.

Empaths have the intrinsic capacity to profoundly comprehend the individuals they are connected with.

They see the hidden inspirations of others' activities, their expectations, and their cravings. It could be said, they are – deliberately or unknowingly – ready to tune into others and to profoundly comprehend them on a passionate level.

Simultaneously, empathic individuals unconsciously receive the feelings and sensations of others.

It's this capacity to profoundly reverberate with others and to take on their lively experiences that cause empaths numerous extraordinary troubles.

This is particularly evident when the empathic individual is not at all mindful of their inborn capacity as well as encircled by poisonous and manipulative individuals.

Empaths are endangered enormously on undesirable mental perspective and sensitive damages.

They might be experiencing ongoing weakness, undeniable degrees of stress, and are overpowered by their significant degree of sensitivity.

Empathic individuals are profoundly touchy to others' sentiments and feelings.

Hence, they unknowingly accept the energy of others and battle extraordinarily with these outside strong influences. Individuals who are naturally empathic are exceptionally touchy to their current circumstance and rapidly get even the smallest chances in others.

Their sensitivity is not simply restricted to actual sensations – it particularly incorporates relational viewpoints. They can "feel into" others and can deeply comprehend their feelings, inspirations, and emotions.

Empaths are very much in contact with their own sentiments and feelings.

They have greatly improved understanding of their own passionate scene than so many others. An empathic individual is adept at interfacing with others.

Simultaneously, it can happen that they associate in a way that is excessively fast with others without taking notice.

One might say, they associate with others on a particular comfort and in a particularly period that others will be unable to follow their speed.

Hence, these individuals may feel as though the empath is excessively fast holding with them, which makes them essentially feels unattached to them.
Empaths mostly see themselves in others. Individuals that are exceptionally empathic are extremely magnanimous as well as tend to put others before themselves.

Empaths are normally inclined to accept that the feelings and desire of others are undeniably more significant than their own special requirements.

A large number of exceptionally empathic individuals are driven by their desire to improve the world in a spot.

They invest significantly more energy with exercises of a compassionate or magnanimous nature than on more conceited ventures.

Another characteristic of empaths is their curiosity. Empaths, every now and again are believed to be away inwardly, unfit to recall things well and thoughtless.

Empathic people are overwhelmed with the feelings of others that they absolutely lose control of themselves in the process.

They are influenced by the disturbed feelings they are entangled with, which regularly drives them to turn out to be completely drenched in emotions and feelings.

Empaths battle within themselves, especially while connecting with numerous individuals or when performing activities they hate.

These two circumstances frequently lead them to turn out to be completely submerged in their own musings.

An empathic individual significantly searches for time alone because it makes them restore their energies. One reason behind this is that they cannot totally loosen up inside seeing others.

They cannot totally deliver themselves in these conditions, which causes it unfathomably hard to totally feel peaceful and pleasing when others are close.

Empathic people are accommodating with others. They are open minded toward others' casualties, shortcomings, and missteps.

They are frequently ready to see themselves in others, which is the reason they treat others compassionate – regardless of whether they do not actually merit it.

To an empathic individual, associating with individuals can be – both intellectually and actually – depleting.
This is particularly obvious when they are with uninformed, little leaning, and self-centered individuals.

In essence, if empathic individuals cannot invest energy with themselves, they seem passionately over-burden.

At the point when an empathic individual is cooperating with others, they may experience battle to separate between others' feelings and their own.

Therefore, they are not generally ready to recognize if certain feelings they experience begin from inside themselves or not. Empathic individuals just cannot stand it to be gone up against with shameful acts.

Empaths at all time focused on individuals who – either purposely or unknowingly – look to deplete their energy.

At the stage when you show profound compassion toward others, their guarded energy goes down, and positive energy replaces it.

That is the point at which you can get more inspirations and ideas in tackling issues. Being an empath comes with numerous difficulties and challenges.

Fortunately, many empaths have figured out how to create powerful techniques that assist them with securing themselves.

One of such procedure is to reflect consistently as it encourages them to be more readily adapt to distressing circumstances to be sure that being an Empath is not equivalent to having compassion.

We are totally brought into the world with sympathy and feelings for one another; Empaths have the capacity to relate to another, yet specifically to comprehend someone else's whole emotions and interaction which ensures certainty and astuteness to the individuals who are attracted to them for help or mending here and there for another.

It's vital for an Empath to completely see every human feeling since it's occasionally important to recognize the feelings of themselves or another.

Knowing where the feeling originates from causes us to control our sentiments in a better limit, not over-respond to them, and afterward set them liberated from our psyches as fast as could really be expected.

For an empath the familiarity with their own feelings and others, just as the arrival of that which is not there is very relevant to driving an upbeat, adjusted and sound way of life.

Being openly places could be dangerous to an Empath: Places like business sectors, arenas, show-room, shopping centers, carnival, mosques, that have heaps of individuals around, can fill the empath with a staggering feeling of emotions coming at them from all areas and without space to move around to try in attempting to work out one feeling from another.

Empaths frequently get amazingly depleted of energy, either from energy vampires or simply taking on a lot from others in a day/week and so forth, which even rest will not help or fix.

Many get determined to have a type of constant weakness disorder.

Although, Empaths characteristic includes mending the capacity inside of them so as to adore just to recuperate others. Anything of a heavenly sort is of extraordinary interest to empaths and they did not get stunned or shocked without any problem.

Empaths need that space to recover from other energies, to maintain equilibrium to themselves and to simply be in their own energy for a positive change. Anything that removes an empath's feeling of opportunity is very weakening and can even have a harmful impact to the states of mind of the detained empath.

Although kind, mindful and sympathetic and frequently more than lenient toward others, empaths do not prefer to be around excessive and pompous individuals for long, particularly the individuals who put themselves first and decline to consider any other individual's emotions or perspectives other than their own.

The adjusted empath distances themselves further a bit from a narcissist, as they understand they cannot help the individuals or even help themselves.

An empath by and large battles to discover themselves much, except if it's to somebody they truly love and trust.

They love to place their energy into finding out about others and holding empathy and care around other's attitudes in the true and legitimate manner. An empath loathes claiming to be upset inside when dismal, this solitary adds to their energy load.

Empaths at times stumble into difficulty for talking reality constantly. Empaths come clean since it feels great to be straightforward, as opposed to simply imagine it does not exist. Empaths get actual manifestations alongside feelings.

Empaths consider all to be creatures as equivalent, and they do not frequently prefer to betray others, regardless of whether at work or in their own lives.

Empathic capacities are a blessing, yet they additionally accompany a bunch of battles. As they are so handily influenced by others' feelings and occupied environmental factors, Empaths do get overwhelmed.

Similar to an empath, you need to build up a solid self-appreciable worth, guard your own cutoff points, and develop a self-care strategy that causes you loosen up and restored.

To remain truly and genuinely strong, you need to sort out some way on yourself as you care for others. Empaths have a significant sensation of understanding that is steadfast and undeniable.

They are equipped for persuading others without obvious actions and can portray what's truly going on underneath the surface. Therefore, empaths struggle recognizing having a place with themselves versus what they associated with and got from another.

This makes life incredibly overpowering. In essence, when an empath develops and sorts out mindfulness, they can build up a worthier level of control and the capacity to decide whose feelings and so forth.

Empaths can encounter outrageous highs and lows which makes them unpredictable.

At a time, they can be distressed and the following moment they can be extremely tragic and remorse.

This is not generally the consequence of how they really feel, but instead, what they have gotten in others, and this can be mistaking for them. Empaths can likewise be requesting for concern — be it for valid justifications or not.

On the other way, Empath believe they are not being heard and they carry on and seem to be penniless, even narcissistic, because of being so overpowered with feeling.

An empath needs to escape from what they are barraged with, or expected to feel associated, and tuned into what could show addictive conduct.

It is essential for an empath to find out about controlling enthusiastic energy, recognize its beginning and apply the rudiments that will permit themselves to push ahead with adjusted health.

Empaths are driven by their interest to comprehend the complexities of life and feel exceptional craving to look for reality and question a bit of everything until they feel comprehended.

Despite the fact that they silence up achievers who like to accomplish the difficult work in the background, empaths are regularly found in places of authority because of their capacity to be engaged, coordinated and strong, fast reasoning and equipped for moving and propelling others with radiant balance.

They are more dependable in giving true recognition upon others instead of tolerating it and regularly found interceding to keep an equilibrium of amicability.

SIGNS OF AN EMPATH

There is nothing out of control with being associated with an empath, nevertheless ignoring it, and dependably setting yourself into conditions where you experience physical or excited misery whereas others provide off a feeling of being fine, will cause immense harm.

Signs of an empath can be associated with feeling exhausted or drained for chaos, energetic instability that cannot be explained by various conditions, extended nature, being looked out among other as a companion (even by dark individual) and so on.

Empaths can promptly get overwhelmed by the emotions and energies of others, and thus need a lot of time alone to invigorate.

This time alone does not have to be truly occupied. Empaths become overwhelmed in gatherings, which can improve their empathy.

Some empaths avoid associations without a doubt as a result of suspicious dread of losing their characters. Wide gatherings are oftentimes overwhelming for empaths in view of the fact that there is such a ton of going on, and unwinding your energy versus someone else's energy.

Empaths are great hearted people and endeavor to mitigate the distress of others. An empath may be a person with the power to induce the mental or energetic state of somebody else.

It comes from the word compassion, that infers the perceptive verification, vicariously experiencing the slants, contemplations, or mindsets of another.

Toward the day's end, you might be an empath if you feel others' emotions or intuitions on a significant level and take them on as your own.

If you have reliably felt more on top of the powerful side of life and what lies under the surface, this could suggest that you are an empath after all.

Without doubtful, notwithstanding, empaths are alleged in holding negative energy, they are going to receive sorrow individuals and wish to assist them with vanquishing issues.

Regardless, empaths will settle for the problems and vibes of others as their own, that is the realization when in doubt feel grieved by all the off-kilter nature on the planet. If you stir on a daily basis feeling such as you expire the load of the planet on your shoulders, you are seemingly an empath.

As a rule, empaths will watch others speak for the length of the day concerning themselves and their life fights, nevertheless once the tables are turned, empaths typically experience problems gap.

Since empaths are additional organized to help others with their problems instead of soaking up isolation, they battle conveying their feelings.

Exactly when you ingest other's energy into your own energy field, you accidentally pass on a huge load of energy with you that can exhaust your own energy levels.

In case you live an operating lifestyle, nevertheless at the same time feel tired regularly, you may be an empath.

In like manner, temporary state will be attributable to energy vampires or those that feed off your energy, coming back to you expressly to exchange their adverse energy for your positive energy.

Making perspective for respectful exercise, show of enquiries, veritable attestation, mental affiliation of managing a problem or perhaps some of miracles that will happen on the planet, you are solely an Empath.

Empaths unremarkably see above the restrictions of overall environmental factors, taking refuge in calm practices, for instance, reflection.

An empath typically needs to get some answers regarding the universe and what lies past the constraints of society taking everything into account.

Empaths have not any issue acquiring new things concerning the world. Empaths frequently become trademark healers (when they planned out how to use their talents fittingly).

This could justify why therefore numerous empaths are force into reasons for living incorporate patching—treatment, teaching, veterinary work, psychiatry, and drug as many in most instances picked fields of labor or study.

All this while, there are some empaths who would like to avoid these trades due to the unbelievable energies annexed to them.

Individuals of unsteady foundations, equally as animals and children, are force into the gleam and real compassion of empaths.

Others might not notice that somebody is an empath, regardless they are going to be force into them as a metal article is to a magnet.

Cutoff points are a certifiable fight for empaths, one clarification being as a result of the foremost half, having to be compelled to fulfill others and not frustrate anyone.

Unfortunately, this suggests they will be taken advantage of by artful people.

Narcissists and empaths attract each other, as narcissists see somebody they can use, and also the empaths see someone they can facilitate and feel.

Being an empath is not easy, you always feel overlooked and disconnected from people. Knowing the signs of an empath can assist you perceive an Empath.

Empathy could be a major part of life. Everybody must have it so as to measure life as an honest human being, while not it, you will find yourself being a douche who's only involved with yourself. However, having sympathy is not similar as being an empath. Knowing the signs of an empath can assist you fathom the difference.

Though reading the signs of an empath is tricky, knowing you are one is super valuable. Not many of us have this ability and once you understand what it is, you will use it to your advantage.

A kid who is mostly equable but susceptible to ostensibly random outbursts may be an empath with specific triggers.

Empaths of all ages wish to look after different people. Unfortunately, they have a tendency to adopt the role of caretaker to an extreme degree, even when doing so places their emotional health in danger.

Raising an empath child can be a challenge, even if you are an empath yourself, their high sensitivity is a gift, but it can also leave them entangled in others.

Being an empath gives you so many advantages over those "regular" folks. While many people struggle with understanding their own life, you are able to see clearly how to guide another to help them live a better life.

There will also be those that do not believe you or your gifts. They are over happy to illustrate everything that might fail with glee.

Several times, they return from an honest place, hoping to avoid wasting you from broken heartedness and failure, however they do not really perceive you or you're calling.

AWAKENED EMPATH

Most individuals have lost their talents to tune into the sentiments of others.

Regardless of our metamorphosed, blistering, artificial societies; our long-held dogmas, culture, beliefs and inner narratives; our physical and emotional diets; our fashion habits, or just our belief that "everything we tend to feel comes directly from us," we have got severely desensitized.

We became basically "sensitivity maimed". We have got to become emotional illiterates. In fact, most of us have become alexithymics – folks that suffer from the shortcoming to real know, and express in words what they are feeling.

We are truly within the most extreme sense, out-of-touch with ourselves and then it's no surprise that once we experience some quite non-secular waking up – when we finally awaken from our "sleep" and a shift in consciousness – we become powerless with not solely our ability to know and feel our own feelings, however our ability to try to do likewise with others.

Suddenly we understand right along that a lot of (not all) of the sentiments that are impeding us up have come as a result of really feeling and seizing the emotions.

Catharsis is important for each empath. In fact, it's essential for every human, despite their level of sensitivity because it dispels a great deal of repressed energy.

For empaths this implies eliminating negative emotional residue from oneself and others. No matter what you do, try and avoid not participating in some style of healthy catharsis.

I have found that changing into lax in our habit of "catharting" has caused chronic pains in our body and ugly mood behaviour.

Good kinds of catharsis model for empaths embrace exercise of any kind, screaming into a pillow, creating a habit of crying each day, happy (laughter therapy), or self-explanation within the style.

When awakened, empaths are capable of seeing the symbolism in situations, checking out what's happening in our bodies, our businesses, and also the world and perceive the deeper meaning.

Once we get chargeable for our gifts and take a step into our future, we bring much-needed harmony back to the current world.

We generally feel as if our ability to envision the goof in others makes us vulnerable. However, this powerful gift, once used with discernment, may be a rare helpful tool.

Everyone has intuition; however the feelings of empaths are quite literal. Our ability to receive intuitive steering us to own a powerful sense of self and respect for self.

Consequently, once we lack shallowness and self-respect, our relationships lack certainty, our intuition is off, and our lives feel as if they are out of our control.

Mastering our energy and emotions, beside trust and respect for ourselves, are a number of the keys to being an empath.

Empaths do not seem to be solely showing gifted emotion, they are psychically attuned as we tend to do.

These hits are available in various ways, like intuition. Since we feel, see, and perceive people on a deeper level, our presence is sort of virtually a healing tonic for hearts in need.
As long as we are shielding this from the world, we will not modify a factor concerning it.

One out of every of our natural gifts is that we have got a refined ability to show concepts into one thing tangible.

Personally, we are combating anxiety, depression, and exhaustion so as to measure up to full potential, we should touch upon the deeper problems that disrupt our daily lives.

It is onerous from wherever you are currently to understand a time your emotions will be balanced, calm, and collected.

It will feel unthinkable to imagine that you simply might get your mental health back or maintain a level of mental state. Be rest assured that though it may seem distant, difficult, undecided or darn close to not possible right now, that it's an ineluctable part of the transformational journey.

Awakened Empath is a comprehensive sign for helping you to develop physical, mental, emotional, and spiritual balance on every level.

Evolving spiritually can be a painful process, as not everyone around you will evolve at the same speed.

We look for new people, more in alignment with who we really are and our new energy. Naturally, we are attracted to these new people, who make us feel good and energized.

We connect with them directly, even virtually, as we are on the same "wave-length".

That's because the connection is from soul to soul. You "see" every other, and you are of identical vibration. It's a heart and soul connection that is possible to be dominated by the ego.

A non-secular wakening is not perpetually the most effective feeling within the world. It will usually be among sturdy feelings of despair and unhappiness once turned into reality and more alert to all the suffering in the world, even depression for a few people.

Once we have a tendency to suddenly "see" and "understand" things, it can generally be a shock.

As an empath, taking care of your own well-being is not enough, you wish to additionally facilitate others to have a positive impact on the world, feeling additional and more compassion and sympathy for others, life solely includes a means after you do one thing for others.

Even if you have got just one person, it requires you to be happy and this makes you feel as if you probably did not come back on earth for nothing, you feel "called" to form something bigger, you cannot go back, and if you generally notice it arduous to be "awaken", you would never want to be.

Being an Empath is awfully a rough ride. Empath wakening concerned healing a large quantity of enmity if however, it "happened".

We speak plenty of empaths associated to be one, however what will it mean to be an empath who has additionally woke up?

An awakened empath is somebody who feels for and loves all, they see the life in everyone, irrespective of wherever their life decisions have taken them.

They sympathized with the supposed "saints" and therefore the "sinners".

They perceive that society, life-choices, environments, and plenty of alternative factors have an impact in molding and shaping everyone and each individual and do no hold any anger or sick towards those that became lost within the darkness.

This includes college shooters, terrorists, murderers, rapists, drunk-drivers, and then on.

Empaths feel pain for all parties concerned as a result of the purity of their soul irrespective of however cloaked it's become.

We grasp there's a break for all to awaken and to seek out our reply of darkness and confusion into the light.

We have a tendency to notice that we are all one which we all express towards each other through our actions, words, thoughts and emotions.

It's challenging being an empath in an exceedingly world crammed with hatred.   It is not easy to take a lazy seat where other points fingers, laugh, mock, and judge others.

It does not matter whether or not the person they are judging is somebody you love, or someone you have never met, you are feeling stormily for that person either way.

Many others have issue understanding this, as a result of lacking flexibility to envision on the far side about their judgements and misbeliefs gained.

I hope that someday, all human race are going to be ready to do this, to rid themselves of many of those misbeliefs and judgements, however till then, empaths should stay strong, stay grounded, and do their best to remain kind and not stray within the madness.

It is incredibly straightforward to help ourselves returning to the defense of others, particularly once we feel others are ganging a private for no matter poor choices.

Have we not all made poor choices? I do know the sensation after you simply need to shake everybody into a deeper understanding.

This is not possible; you only end up turning into someone who judges. In all, we have a tendency to stray in judging others who judge.

Then we become as lost as they do, and to envision ourselves as better as additional understanding, as "saints".

We all know this is often not true, we know that irrespective of who is speaking, judging, hating, or loving, we are all one and therefore the same.

We all start out as stunning little bundles of sunshine and become shrouded with misbeliefs, perceptions, social judgements, morals and values that do not align with our soul's truth.

If you are wakening empath, be sure you simply do not seem to be alone.

There are several people out there rummaging identical issues, coping with the same overwhelming feelings, and making an attempt to form sense of it all.

The gift of an empath is commonly misbranded as a curse. This is often not in the slightest degree true. It's going to be troublesome within the world if we have a tendency to board today, however it's a gorgeous factor to possess this gift.

Empath are an intuitive, loving, soul-connected individual. Empath possess the sunshine that such a large amount of others is seeking, guide by words, actions, associated love.

We have a tendency to the pavers of light, we birth the steppingstones down the trail towards understanding and unconditional love.
Awakening to the reality that you simply may probably be an Empath could come backs in waves, it's going to come as a fast feeling of unity or it may come as a gradual feeling over certain time, it's going to leave you feeling confused every now and then as a result, of all of it may be very new and alarming to you as a recall to woke up Empath.

Once awakening, everything around might begin to look terribly completely different and you tend to envision everything with a new perspective, everything that once seemed absolutely logical to you may not have identical impact and therefore gain additional insight into things that may not have meant abundant for you before.

Although the Empath could be a stunning religious affair, it additionally comes with several ups and downs.

Therefore, it's nearly necessary for every woke up Empath to journey through the paths of ups and downs to actually shed themselves of any previous pain they might have encountered in their lives.

This shedding also permits for inner healing that require the Empath begin the cycle of healing themselves.

Empath become more intuned with their universal energy, they received messages more clearly and execute new energy in a very positive manner.

As an Empaths, you are feeling more inclined to measure your life in a healthy, peaceful and uncomplicated manner than before and should have a more holistic outlook, as your own self-healing to utilize the maximum amount as its needed, you recognize that inner peace will solely be found among oneself, and not within the materialistic ways in the world and similarly ready to differentiate on a more universal level what the world have to repair that has gone wrong and notice solace through causation healing.

When awakened, empaths are capable of seeing the symbolism in situations. Empaths are able to cross-check what's happening in our bodies, our businesses, and therefore the world and understand the deeper meaning.

Empath's awareness has been on the increase. This appears to been greatly perpetuated by the actual fact that most people felt lost or disconnected from society and that we required to grasp.

The Empath's awakening seems to be similar from one person to the next. For most, it happens once during dark times, or after we begin to 'work on ourselves'.

Empaths might begin a meditation to assist contend with a way of disconnect, or follow a vocation to review metaphysical or holistic subjects as some way to realize a bigger understanding of life or to become a far better person, however after adopting new ways in which of being, or gap up their awareness, triggered strange physical connection.

Well, as an Empath, we have invariably felt the emotions and energy of others (often while not realizing), but when we have a tendency to begin performing on ourselves, we come back to sense.

The incontrovertible fact that numerous Empaths are raising now, shows us that it's for a reason.

We have a tendency to have a purpose and enablement to try and do. we have a tendency to scattered everywhere in the world to do our work from our own very little corner.

We have a tendency to keep pressing forwards, onward and upwards to engaged and strengthen our energy and that of others around us. As long as we still work on ourselves and keep in awareness, we continue to evolve as Empaths.

Empaths awareness of higher level of consciousness collapse to interactions with different realities and dimensions.

TRIGGERS FOR EMPATHS

Empath triggers cause a touchy individual or empathic individual to feel partner over-burden bringing about tension, gloom, and enthusiastic depletion.

The mental condition of an Empath just alteration with a choice bearing positive reaction once encountering extreme boosts.

These reactions mostly result into post horrendous issue when intensed conditions happen. Nevertheless, an empath's brain can deliver a riotous winding of feelings, exacting extraordinary trouble.

In such scenario, an empath feels an enthusiastic over-burden at the smallest occurrence. This especially occurs if the individual does not have any assortment over undesirable feelings.

The psyche of an empath is an unrealistically uncommon one. Relatively few of us really see the idea strategy of someone so mindful, sympathetic, and sacrificial.

At the point when an empath has the vigorous need to feel misjudged, this will lead them to feeling doltish and without a doubt "insane".

To the misconstrued empath, you should comprehend that you simply are not insane or unusual.

Truth be told, your capacity to pull out into the feelings of others is a huge blessing, you have enthusiastic knowledge. At the point when someone encounters relinquishment in the course of their life, they are probably going to feel undesirable by any individual or gathering.

Recollect that everyone has worth and reason; especially you, you have that extraordinary force of really getting feelings, the planet needs you.

To be blond by someone is the most unadulterated human aptitude to exist.

An individual who are survivors of passionate conditions will in general cover from the overall population to prevent any damages and agonies to their feeling of brain.

Actually, you were adored from the moment you were conceived by somebody. In all honesty, there are people need that may not exclusively be, for example, you wishing they could be blond by you. They had the chance to feel adored as characteristic.

In this case, you cannot empower it to interfere with you down at whatever your sentiments are not responded.

Every skill has planned you on the grounds of the individual you are today, making you sweet in such a ton of ways.

On the off chance that you are caring empathic towards others, those characteristics alone reason you in everything about first adorable and respected creatures.

For an empath, the need to feel acknowledged will be solid. Empaths are in this way loving and caring that they anticipate those equivalent emotions from others.

For most, they join the sensation of acknowledgment with additionally feeling comprehended, needed, esteemed, and adored.

At the point when we feel dismissal, it's simple for our good and self-contemplations to cleared away by a dim ocean of feeling. Make sure to focus on those connections who are as of now brimming with adoration, acknowledgment, and worth. At the point when an empath is advised to "get more than" a horrendous hurt or weighty feelings, they feel as though their feelings are excessively absurd.

We hear these words and think, "What's up with me?. What people without compassion neglect to comprehend is that it's difficult to "get over" hurt.

Truly, you can strive to push ahead with an end goal to oversee your life, yet it's not something that occurs over time. Being an empath intends to emphatically feel for other people, however to unequivocally feel for ourselves and the things we have encountered.

For the confounded empath, do not suppress your feelings or shroud horrendous encounters. The high affectability you experience is for an explanation, you were intended to discuss these things.

Empaths are world transformers; do not empower anybody to disparage you into suspecting something.

As people, we are molded to develop further from horrible pains.

When you accept the capacity of the human psyche and the manner in which flexible it becomes while encountering sure occasions, you may see that you simply will develop through these in turn, you will get more grounded than anything .

There's no opportunity to "get over" anything, exclusively to move forward. In a situation that starts a personal issue in you knowingly or accidentally, constantly keep in mind that you simply were created for this reason.

Empaths see the world differently than other people; they are keenly aware of others, their pain, and what they need emotionally but it's not just emotions.

For the Empath, feeling other people's energy and emotions is normal, both negative and positive.

These 'trigger' people tend to spew dark, angry energy and refuse to accept or change their behaviour, even if it has been pointed out to them how their ways affect others.

They tend to find fault in everyone (except themselves) and choose not to see the good in those around them.

It is not just negative people who activate painful responses within the Empath and thus become triggers. Anyone who is suffering emotionally can ignite the Empath's pain body.

This normally happens when others pain is something to which you can relate to or have experienced. Feeling their pain can take you back to the time of your own loss and activates the memory of grief.

However, these responses unremarkably cut back as their emotional pain subsides.

A trauma response is kindled when the person, acting as a trigger, is arbitrarily mentioned in conversation, seen from a distance or one thing reminds you of them.

Basically, on every occasion aforementioned, person comes into your energy field through thought, word or presence which is enough to activate a reaction.

The trigger is also easy however the reaction is commonly traumatic. Empath will avoid trauma-trigger-people but cannot continuously stop them from connecting with them.

The most effective methods to contend with them, is by continued to follow your chosen strategies of safety, keep grounded connection in alignment among the mind, body and spirit.

Emotional triggers are those super-reactive places inside you that become activated by somebody else's behaviors or comments.

When triggered, you either withdraw showing emotion and easily feel hurt or maybe respond in an aggressive approach.

Your reaction is therefore intense as a result of defensive against a particularly painful feeling that has surfaced.

Your emotional triggers are wounds that require to heal. These beliefs are supported fears and that they are not reality, you do not wish to be oftentimes triggered, nobody does.

It's exhausting associated painful, particularly for sensitive and empathetic individuals as a result of empaths are finely tuned instruments once it involves emotions.

They feel everything, typically to an extreme, and are less apt to intellectualize feelings. Intuition is the filter through that they experience in the world.

Empaths tend to soak up energy concerning problems that they need not resolved simply and deeper than others.

To heal your emotional triggers, you want to begin with compassion and examine any beliefs that you have carried around from your family or society, you wish to start gently addressing the elements of yourself that feel flawed, equivalent to doubts regarding your body image or search out once you heal the initial trauma or false belief, you set yourself showing emotion free, then you will not become as simply triggered or drained within the future.

Empaths are vulnerable to fight the emotional or physical pain that they need not found out in themselves.

The more they heal problems that trigger them, the less seemingly they will be to absorb emotions from others.

They might sense them however they would not cut as deeply or drain them. Distinguishing emotional triggers causes you to be most upset and thrown off balance than any others.

Studies regarding these triggers originated as knowing where your triggers come back from permitting you to understand yourself better.
It painful to come back to previous memories, so do so gently, and cue yourself in all part of the healing process.

This will assist you substitute the negative belief with a positive, a lot of realistic decision to mind your positive mantra whenever negative thoughts creep in.

Once empaths absorb the impact of disagreeable emotions, it will trigger panic attacks, depression, food, sex and drug binges, and inordinateness of physical symptoms that defy ancient diagnosing from fatigue to agoraphobia.

Empaths will be triggered by the tiniest of visuals or words, and this news simply happens to contain a cesspit of them. Living or operating in an exceedingly surroundings also triggers tension among the body.

For an empath, walking into a thronged space can feel overwhelming as talking to individual who is upset or unhappy will be demanding.

Loud noises, powerful scents, and bright lights can be over stimulating.

MANAGING TRIGGERS

The ideas in managing your triggers is to understand the events, situations, thoughts, or recollections that trigger symptoms comparable to anger or impulsiveness.

There are exercises you will be able to work out what your triggers are. Once you have got known your triggers, you can understand the way to influence them.

You can start by determinative whether or not a selected trigger may be avoided. Several triggers, however, cannot be avoided easily.

If you discover that some triggers cannot be avoided, you can learn to cope with them by developing an action plan, seeing a therapist, and working on approaching your triggers gradually.

Being an Empaths is an improbable issue however it may be terribly exhausting at a similar time.

If you stop what specialize in your feeling and defrayal time on yourself, the additional reason you would like to shield yourself and ensuring you are not perpetually drawing in negative. By meditating everyday, you are setting yourself up to be at your strongest.

It offers you some alone time wherever you are not studying on the energies of others.

The time is use to withdraw deep into yourself, experience your own energy and understand your own feeling. Being an Empaths, you may notice that almost all of your energy gets taken on smaller issue.

This suggests whereas you are exploiting energy to negativity, you are using way not up to what you would if you were to let that energy in completely.

Being an ineffective empath who is unaware of their empath triggers have unfortunate influence, that makes them ineffective.

That's why understanding our empath triggers is so important. Once we spot them, we can begin responding to them appropriately.

Simply being physically on the brink of somebody can cause us to tune into them emotionally. This is especially tough in thronged places comparable to looking malls or at work. To make things worse, several impaired Empaths experience unconscious triggers: they will be triggered while not realizing it.

All of a sudden, they feel stinky and they do not realize why. Most empaths suppresses the emotional noise they devour from others which is "normal," and they just ought to strengthen up.

We learn to regulate our response to empath triggers. It can be stunning to understand however how often we are being triggered while not realizing it.

It's like being perpetually poked by an invisible stick. However, knowing when we are becoming triggered permits us to try and do one thing regarding it.

Instead of a helpless victim to a strategy we will not control, we can finally take charge. It's no secret that life can feel arduous at times.

This can be very true for empaths, who tend to be deeply stricken by the energy of those around them.

It is very important for your own spiritual, emotional, and physical well-being that are just unharness toxicity in your life and take away yourself from adding value to yourself appropriately, get lots of exercise and rest, and keep hydrated.

You are far better ready to influence everything that comes with being an empath if you are physically as healthy as you will be able to be.

This may assist you feel additional up to the mark of your own life and feelings.

EMPOWERED EMPATH

There are unimaginable overlaps within the traits, capacities and experiences that empaths share that are undeniable.

Empaths notice that they are additional usually right than they are wrong – and as they learn from their life experiences, what they dismiss as "paranoia" prove to be correct reflections of what others miss in their hurry to form selections.

Empowered empaths learn to honor their skills and use them with confidence; they do not need validation from outside sources to follow their instincts, they are going for it and once they do, they sometimes succeed and cause others around them to marvel however they could even need to risk maltreatment within the process.

Actually authorized empaths learn that this risk is worthwhile – as a result of the opposite risk would mean sacrificing who they honestly are and what they understand inside to be.

Malignant narcissists continuously tend to feed on empaths because it's been discovered that they know that there's lots of energy, materials, resources and support.
Empaths enhance the energy of those around them with the wealth of their emotional labor and talent to honor different perspectives.

47

Narcissists see that special gift in empaths and they get to closed to them and receive the resources of the empath that might additional aid their agenda.

Toxic folks use empaths as the simplest way to short circuit their plans to success and circumvent their own like for healing.

They use the compassion of empaths to urge away with their deadly behavior while not being command in charge of it; they exploit their disposition to adapt and their resilience to ensnare them into an abuse cycle; they get pleasure from being associated with a kind-hearted, compassionate individual to lift their social capital and value.

They feast on the generosity of empaths as if it were a daily meal, while not having to administer abundant reciprocally.

Empowered empaths understand they are not chargeable for somebody else's harmful behavior; they shrewdness to indicate compassion from a distance if they have to; and most importantly, they honor themselves enough to care for and expect reciprocity as a must.

They know how to have interaction in radical self-care, with the complete conviction that they learn to worry for themselves, the more they need to administer.

The strange factor concerning empaths is that they will get even the foremost person to open up and tell their account in seconds.

This is because empaths usually have broken hearts, they continue to be open-hearted by nature. People intuitively trust them because they conjointly tend to wear their hearts on their sleeves.

Even the most showing emotion closed off empath slivers of open-heartedness, bright light-weight crawling out from the crevices of their person, which invite individual to share their darkness.

From a non-secular perspective, empaths are natural healers and their birthright is healing.

They get this world to heal, to heal themselves which might build them vulnerable to deadly sorts wanting to take advantage of their energy for his or her own agenda.

Conversations with an empath healing on each side end in exhaustion for the empath, if an empath is not totally authorized.

The darkness of this ability is that empaths carry vast power to assist in healing, they usually forget to heal themselves within the process. In contrast to somebody who is not an empath, even the fastest of social interactions, if they are showing emotion loaded from input from the opposite person, will result in fast action.

There should be a form of "cleansing of the psyche" that has to present itself when even only one interaction and words sometimes need to be said to safeguard.

Empaths acting with certainty have incredibly advantage in instituting sound relationship from the earliest starting point as they probably are aware themselves better, they likewise realize which weight is theirs to convey.

In addition, they finish their limits and can cut off harmful connections before they get an opportunity to heighten. They have a tremendous measure of force; however, they generally do not have a clue how to claim it.

Empaths possessed tuned instruments; they are sharp in their instinct, their capacity to get things going and in their "knowing" which makes them unimaginable manifestos when they are completely engaged.

They will primarily show everything while not exception, to that extent as they fathom the way to relinquish their association connected with monumental dreams which quicken for empaths at a worrisome rate; wealth are available large waves; love and appreciation which flood their lives, within the event that they are available to.

Empaths flourish once they satisfy the targets and points their brain to deeply adjust.

Being happy claiming the hugeness of their force maybe the best obstacle an empath has to encounter to accomplish at the final which were meant to; nonetheless once they realize it is related to the additional assertion recuperating of the world, they will not be patient to wander out on a more outstanding mission whereas typifying the magnificence of their actual own or leftover spirited vibes from others which leave them effectively depleted.

Their feelings are essential for his or her terribly own complicated insights, the discernments, responses and feelings of others around them, even as their own feelings towards the way with others.

Empaths most obligation lies in recuperating themselves, simply once they are utterly enabled will they need the choice to assist in the mending excursion of others.

Enabled empaths figure out how to quit saying 'sorry' for their cravings and perceive the legitimacy of claiming them with full power.

They figure out how to envision their own feelings and set themselves up intellectually for whatever is to come.

Above all of all, empaths should discover that they are permitted to claim their shadows – the most obscure pieces of themselves incredible by understanding how to effectively coordinate different parts of themselves.

This does not mean surrendering to that obscurity, yet utilizing it as fuel to make additional light-weight on the world rather than subduing it.

Suppression simply prompts carrying these spirited sicknesses to the surface, because it may offer them a more outstanding chance to be conferred to medication and for every engaged empath, there's a resurrection once they fathom the way to be their legitimate selves notably when they rotate the planet once more as creatures who utterly stand for all that produces ground-breaking in any case.

An empath emits an improbable and enthusiastic spirit of adoration, light and brilliance, but the hearth probably completely seethes when an empath exists in an exceedingly spot within which they need a way of safety enough to shine.

Empaths are delicate, sensitive and massively weak human within, and once injured on their actual feelings, they normally get obvious and enormous.

Regarding an Empath, being harmed once makes them general show up additional delicate in most instances which influences their help or satisfaction, thinking that its laborious and testing to relinquish substantial offends to them and gaining ground in additional correspondence where their inclination has been upset.

The foremost ideal approach to utterly accompany an empath is by creating a protected and powerful stage to assemble a future upon. Within the event that show up through question and misdirection, it will end up to be massively laborious to repair them.

Empaths blossom with trust, dependableness and constancy. Show them this stuff and their relationship are extraordinarily hard to break.

As empaths are exceptionally energetic individuals, they frequently find a solid interaction with a diversion or premium that others will discover.

Due to their creative side, they find a resonance with music, dance, writing, art, activism, reading, meditation, humanitarian causes or other similar interests.

Whatever it is that has captured the mind of an empath become sacred in their hearts.

Although they will have a deep attachment to their passions, it is far easier to understand that an empath loves all things at great levels of intensity and they need outside interests to survive and feel alive, this can sometimes be difficult for others to understand.

As empaths are sensitive to energy, their worst-case scenarios are confrontations and aggressive situations.

Although under normal circumstances they are one of the least violent and aggressive characters, they can easily lose their self-control if they become absorbed in the negative and toxic energy that surrounds them.

At times it may feel like being in the company of a magically gifted being who has special powers that have been led to believe do not exist within humans.

This can be both a blessing and a curse. Nothing will get past an empath as they see, feel and connect with everything at all times.

Empowered empaths who step into leadership positions in their families and communities can be strong diplomats for peace, truth, and positive change.

DARK SIDE OF BEING AN EMPATH

The darkest side of being an empath comes as two restricting powers that exist in an empath's spirit.

Consistently, empaths can feel both the great and the terrible vibrations around them.

The clouded side and the power for daily routine existed together in an empath's heart.

Empaths are individuals who live to provide for the others, exist in amicability with the world, and ability to tune into their companions.

Through various challenges, they are consistently there to help. Empaths are typically those with exceptional emotions who not just sense entirely unexpected energies but are prepared to skill them.

Notwithstanding, for the empaths, there are two parts of the coin. For them conveying the dark side of their abilities may demonstrate hefty.
From one perspective, the abilities of empaths construct others to have a sense of security and accordingly, empaths are the individuals who assemble the premier significant relationship.

At times, empaths may feel overwhelmed by either choice. As a rule, these individuals are somewhat more touchy to the negative things around them.

An empath's life is gagged with all the contentions between shrewd partner underhanded that everyone around them are experiencing.

Tragically, empaths ordinarily concede destruction to all or the agony they assimilate.

The best methodology for an empath is to try not to squander themselves from implosion to shield their spirit from the steady progression of human feelings.

Empaths should conjointly give a ton of consideration to their emotions. Empaths' dull viewpoint is excruciating to convey. As they are consistently so engrossed with serving to other people, empaths generally toss their own feelings.

Accordingly, they continue to convey the contrary's distress on their unselfish toes for their entire life.

For their own sentiments, empaths ought to see and note that managing the issues of others is not what they need to re-visit in this world. In an attempt to keep away from compassion which overwhelm the other part of their life, Empath should not concede all of themselves to everyone that discovered their way.

They ought to conjointly crush the dividers including their heart so they will empower their empathic selves to attempt to savvy in their own lives also.

The dull part of Empath includes you giving and providing for different people while not understanding that you simply are out of your own because of you are not turning your inward character.

You do not appear to be the most extreme as add up to yourself as you are to other people, you result into passionate fascination, exhausted, unpleasant and feeling like never going to budge.

This happens once you understand it difficult to disregard other people feelings and remaining devoted yourself on the amount that you are happy to give and specifically have not taken in a manner to flip all that warm goodness toward yourself and say "presently even to the hurt of yourself, you wrap up others' satisfaction before your own because of the torments you feel.

You have not been prepared to moor realizing that it's at least not your duty to make them upbeat and you have not in any way finished what just cannot amazingly satisfy them.

No issue with regards to whatever you provide for others, they will generally require a great deal of expert if they figure out how to give.

It's simply similar to the past assertion that "you give a man a fish and he hurl for a day, you train an individual to fish he eats for a lifetime".

At the point when you are never-endingly assuming liability for others', you wrap up instructing them to consider you.

You are making a mutually dependent relationship any place as the contrary individual gets reliant upon you for their bliss and you are taking it on your shoulders to remain renewal to their satisfaction. You may give this a shot of affection, anyway it lands up harming different people because they never discover how to top off their own because of the need to remain cheerful to others and to try not to make them awkward (or cause them any torment) you wrap up making others' assessments a ton of indispensable than you, as you end up requesting for conclusions since you have gotten in this way outside of yourself whether you are not doing "great job" of making others cheerful.

You become so focused on others and the manner in which they feel you interfacing with what you feel, what you really want, what you eventually get.

You find yourself oral communication "I do not even understand what I prefer anymore" as a result of ensuring everybody else is okay, creating them happy, prioritizing their opinions, and making sure nobody else is uncomfortable.

There's no area for you left after you are taking all of your energy and use it outward as alternative people's lives all the time.

Without knowing a way to set firm boundaries and deeply connect with whom you are and what you want, you will end up chasing around what they need and the way they feel and they will understand that they will manipulate you with a frown, a tear, or a raised.

This is why empaths find yourself in relationships with narcissists, sociopaths, and abusive people.

They thought they can fix them and heal them. It comes from a decent place; however it ultimately lands up resulting in the empath feeling like they need fully lost control over their life.

Being a sensitive empath requires a lot of potential downsides. When an individual is licitly happy, glowing and simply beaming from being happy in their life they impact the lives around them while not trying.

Other people are raised up by simply their presence. We have got all been around somebody like that before; someone who causes you to feel loved.

Not as a result of their continuously putting other desires first, however just in virtue of who they are. When you place your own happiness first and foremost this is what happens.

The positive effects on others truly amplifies and expands. You do not seem to be abandoning people, you are changing into a model for a way life can work when you are self-sustaining merrily and satisfactorily. Not everybody can afford it though, let's be real. Some individuals will want you to still carry the burden of their happiness.

Being an empath includes a ton of potential downsides however there is need to assure you that it's one amongst the foremost powerfully positive gifts you would have.

It simply takes time and talent to understand a way to navigate this ability.

Empaths helped many people navigate their own actions and feel stronger, anchored into their own happiness, understand how to yield people-pleasing, and eventually understand themselves at all times.

This improves relationships, businesses, friendships, money situations.

The dark aspect of being an empath is that they are enclosed by negative energy and negative people of the world.

As a result, the laws of nature direct empaths to assist and maintain the "balance" of humanity.

To any or all empaths out there, you are loved, you are sturdy and also the planet is therefore lucky to own you.

The dark side of sympathy is not detected or talked concerning yet, it exists and might poison an empath's life.

Sympathy is the capability to be ready to place oneself into another person's shoes and perceive their thoughts and feelings.

An empath may be one that has the flexibility to resonate with alternative people, on many various levels, in order that they will accurately feel it's not nevertheless renowned, however empaths have this ability and believe that it is innate and is bimanual down through our DNA.

Empaths are generally considered being sympathetic, caring, sensitive to the emotions of others, and compassionate souls.

The terribly nature of empathy means that many of us trust empaths for support and guidance.

It additionally implies that empaths see more of the planet than we have a tendency to do, and as such, this could cause issues in numerous areas.

The dark aspect of Empath is that they cannot handle their own emotions as they supposed; an empath is well-versed in emotions that they would be consultants in handling their own emotions, however the reality is that they are in a very constant battle to those emotions under control as a result of feeling others' emotions so keenly, significantly others' sadness, it can generally bring them blooming down.

Empath realize it onerous to differentiate between their own emotions and alternatives' and have to be compelled to find other empathy to share.

Empaths are significantly at risk of negative energy, as this upsets them greatly.

When all they sense is negative energy, they can fleetly become spent as a result of empaths are trusting souls who perpetually believe the faces of people.

When an empath finds out that they need been conned, they can simply make up a deep depression.

As empaths value offers to other instead of receiving, they are more possible to neglect their own welfare, together with their mind and body.

This is the dark aspect that's only too common, as empaths are fatigued from the strain of what they experience, is it only too simple to forget to require care.

Empaths notices it arduous for them to fall soft because empath has seen all the cruelty within the world, they find it extraordinarily troublesome to convey themselves as a whole.

They hold a bit piece of their heart back, simply just in case they are attending to be hurt in the future, they cannot allow themselves to fall deeply in love because they are terrified of experiencing all that passion, it might be an excessive amount pressure on them.

They usually want to carry an important burden. Empaths are altruistic people that are bombarded by sensory information on a daily basis.

They feel that their role in life is to assist others, however this places a vast burden on them, as they cannot presumably help everybody that they are available.

Despite the danger to themselves, they might still rather carry another's person's challenges than let that person down.

Empaths ought to realize that the issues of the globe are not theirs to solve.

To stop the dark aspect of empath from taking on their life, they are not ought to offer themselves to each single person they meet.

At a similar time, they ought to disenchant the walls of their heart once a while.

The world might not understand; however the empath comprehends it only too well; the darkness that comes from having this unaccountable gift.

A pain and disappointment that's distinctive to people who feel every vibration of energy around them as if 1,000,000 fingers were plucking the little these folks understand that, on the inside, you are a raging ball of contrastive feelings, all wooly-minded along to make an incomprehensible and endless noise that you simply struggle to silence.

Sometimes it's thus overwhelming that it sounds like an invisible hand is clasped tight around your neck; a pressure so intense that it takes each ounce of your strength.

The sharp and negative shifts in energy are the worst as a result of being available whole out of the blue and provide you with very little time to prepare.

They hit you with a freight train, dynamical you into a spiral of confusion, desolation, and distress.

Sadly, it's the negative energy that you simply feel the most, and it's solely created worse by the world you see around you.

The suffering, the heartache, and also the malevolent forces that causes it plague on you much more than the good, and the benevolent will elevate you up.

It is each physically and mentally exhausting to measure your life in a nearly constant state of heightened emotion, however you hold it along principally to convey a composed, if typically, a bit.

Yet you cannot resist the temptation to undertake to assist others; it's your terribly nature to show your attention to the ills and wishes of those in hassle as a result of somehow feeling that serve to them.

The dark aspect need not win out forever. You can, with some practice, and with the support of those who love you, learn to modify the piercing severity of the emotions you experience.

Your pain and hurt will be eased, and you will learn to acknowledge that feelings which are yours and which come back from external energy sources, you would like not put up your guard perpetually up; there's how to let others in while not turning into powerless by what you do.

It comes through acceptance, earnest effort, and also the sheer can and determine to not let your prized quality become your womb-to-tomb prison.

Never provide up, never give in. Being an empath can cause somebody to be naturally giving, spiritually-attuned, and a wonderful listener.

This can build anyone to engulf, feel weary or to become unhappy.

The opposite of an Empath do not seem to be usually displayed, however they are vital to understand, particularly if you are in a relationship with an empath.

The dark aspect of being an empath stems from having two perpetually conflicting voices within their head. It's common for an empath to become powerless from invariably feeling each good and also the bad, the negative and the positive.

The dark side of being an empath comes from the actual fact that they need to be willing to neglect their own body and mind for the sake of others.

Neglecting yourself for an extended amount of your time can cause you to feel lost and isolated.

Several empaths find themselves desperate to persist a self-examination journey each few years so as to reconnect with their own body and soul.

The dark aspect of being an empath is the war that's perpetually waged within.

They strive as arduous as they will to fight the sadness, the darkness, and also the pain they feel, in order to not let it bring them down into a spiral.

They got to learn the way to differentiate between their own emotions and false emotional energies.

This technique keeps their emotions in restraint to seek out others who understand them, those who they will consult with which will really listen.

Empaths have this incomprehensible gift that comes with a high value and plenty of cons. 'No' is much too rude for an empath to talk and is not recognized in their vocabulary.

As a result, the empath permits itself to be manipulated, used, and abused however still believes they are doing it for a bigger sensible and utmost purpose.

The empaths do not simply drive the darkness away however absorb it and confine it inside them.

An empath suffers in silence, irrespective of what proportion comes smothering from the hands of darkness around his throat, still smiles, and is often able to extend his hands for help. It takes his strength to not give up to the darkness.

There may be a dark side of an empath. Empaths has his demons to fight, his flaws to correct and depression to deal with, they does not need a private tragedy for them to suffer.

With keeping everything you have in your heart to yourself then adding thereto everything others have in their hearts too. They carry the load on their unselfish shoulders. Empaths got to be able to disenchanted the wall they need designed up around their feelings so they will let their sympathetic selves benefit in their own life.

Otherwise, empaths are destined to fight a war inside themselves that never ends.

The dark side of being an empath is not knowing that being so selfless places an implausibly significant burden on one's self. Even the empaths that do acknowledge the heavy nature of their selflessness often like better to highly favor, as a result of carrying that is more significant than least it falls on somebody else's shoulders.

Growing up in this world as an empath will be very difficult, not only do they face being known as "too sensitive" however they are not given the tools.

Therefore, the sole alternative choice is to become cold and callous. Once you feel, absorb and embody all of the emotions around you, heartlessness can act as a defense mechanism.

It can appear a logical option to shut yourself far from the world. Several, their sympathetic sense are activated in childhood, empaths are born with nervous systems that are already super sensitive so living in a very home setting that's disagreeable or anxiety causation like thunder for the empath, their empathic talents act because the defence in a nuclear family needs them to invariably air.

Our sensitivity that is supposed to shield us and alert us to danger, finishes up operating against us and solely intensifying the anxiety or danger we tend.

It's for this reason that empaths are usually diagnosed as to anxious or depressed as a result of their system being perpetually overladen and cannot relax.

We tend not to seem to be given the right tools to manage our nervous system and convey peace to our bodies.

Serving to others whereas you have got your own issues is completely exhausting, particularly if you are an empath.

PITFALL OF ANGER FOR EMPATHS

Of all the feelings that empaths experience, the foremost powerful and probably damaging feeling is anger.

Of course, anger may be destructive to everyone, except for the empath it can be particularly potent.

The reason for this can be that empaths feel first and react, then suppress later. There are lot of intense emotion which are deeper than the interaction.

The initial response for empaths is either to react with equal force to the anger, which frequently involves awfully intense and potentially ruinous outburst, or for the introspective empath to run or scarper the immediate space.

Many of those sensitive souls burst into tears at what seems to be inappropriate moments for no reason.

Wherever there's anger, there could be always pain beneath as a result, it's quite common for empaths to remember feelings, emotions or situations, before others are aware themselves, anger becomes terribly expressed.

If the oppressed individual is a partner in an exceedingly romantic relationship, anger will become a land mark.

An experiences a degree of extreme stress sort of a caged tiger – pacing, miserable and simply waiting to pounce, or escape.

Unpleasant problems, open sore of the skins, hypertension, low morale, inability to sleep, lack of power to push through are physical symptoms of an empath who will not manage a powerful feeling of annoyance or feelings infuriated in the mind.

Being infuriated perpetually makes them have nice emotional weights that later results into acerbity or displeasure – wholly not palatable.

New feelings of hurt and discomfort encompasses a great impact on their feelings, like been terribly near to fire.

First and foremost, anger is usually at the core regarding fear. If you as an empath can take a breath and go beyond the surface repeatedly you may feel the shift to concern.

The anger is simply acting sort of a defend from fear or further pain. It's no potential to damage you unless you step into its direct path; take it on as your own; or feed it along with your own reactions and emotions thinking as a hearth that needs gas to breath.

Empaths are precocious healers and their calm reaction to anger will have awfully powerful impact on others, additionally as themselves.

You as an empath should calm yourself first and the fastest way to do this is to remind yourself that is not coming from you, but through you.

This allows you to step back and observe what you are feeling, seeing and cut to the root of it.

Empaths do feel jealousy, anger and all the emotions "regular" people feel. Empaths are not superhuman.

They are regular people who feel more deeply than others, and they may also have other abilities.

Empaths are human and anger is part of human feelings. It may seem like an excuse to disown unpleasant feelings but it's not.

Mess with an empath long enough still do what they unremarkably do - they absorb the feelings.

Some individuals would like to learn the way to be empathic, whereas others would love to learn how to retain the most effective components of that skill, while managing the tougher people who get angry or unhappy at you or with you if you are not doing what they need you to do, however it's necessary to recollect that their feelings do not seem to be your feelings, and your well-being is not addicted to them.

Sometimes an empath can understand what they have to say or do to create sensible boundaries, however have a tough time following through and expressing it.

When you are the one that feels suffering over anyone around you, it's hard to not feel chargeable for remedying it.

Having the ability to urge in reality along with your suppressed anger, you will be able to unharness it in an exceedingly safe and delicate approach like victimizing sound which is very important for long-run health and when empaths begin to own a lot more anger outbursts, the body is telling us to 'pay attention', as a result of one thing is off.

One thing has to be when you focus into what the anger is attempting to inform you, often what you will find is your body telling you that a private boundary has been violated, or that something in your life needs to be examined.

There may be serious long-run health consequences of hidden emotional stress like suppressed anger that go unbridled in your body; we all know that there's often a link between chronic health conditions and suppressed one.

We additionally know that there's often a link between suppressed anger and clinical depression.

The volatility of anger typically caught an empath unaware. When an individual is angry or sad, that undulation energy shoots out.

The energy truly goes quite distance. If the energy hits an empath, the empath suddenly feel hurt or sad, that's as a result of an empath somehow has the biological ability to raised faucet into energy fields than most people.

Because an empath is in a position to feel vibrational energies, an empath sometimes struggles with keeping a balanced feeling state of mind.

Anger is the initial emotion we usually feel once we understand we have got been unjustly treated.

OVERWHELMED EMPATHS

It is easy for empaths to become increasingly overwhelmed by their feelings in their life. But it's important for empaths to figure out the best ways to handle their emotions.

Empaths go through so many emotions in one day. When you have that extra emotional sensitivity, it might feel impossible to be happy.

Each empath handles their emotions differently. Even, if you have just figured out you are an empath, you may need some guidance on how to be happy and handle your emotional sensitivity.

Working through emotions is a very important part of life for an empath as a result of, while not it, empaths become too inundated to be productive and stable.

So, for empaths, there are voluminous steps to truly operating through their emotions so that they will realize happiness in life.

Limiting it slow with showing emotion debilitating, individual assist you feel happier as an entire because you may not be taken advantage of and that they will not be ready to drain the maximum amount of energy out of you as they would if you spent your usual time.

Empaths undoubtedly get overwhelmed by loud noises, music, and yelling.

They have quietness to be able to think things through well while not being distracted. In a very romantic relationship, an empath can attempt with intimacy.

Empaths simply become defeated and might desire they are losing themselves so they pull back. Empaths need clear boundaries in relationships.

Since empaths are to bear with their emotions, they are secure and show emotion snug in surroundings to figure in that their time at work does not drain them of all their energy.

Empaths can become inundated and overstimulated to their extreme sensitivity.

Empaths become overwhelmed in crowds, which might amplify their empathy.

They tend to be self-examining and like one to one contact or connection.

Though an empath are extroverted, they like limiting what quantity time they will be in a crowd or at a party.

Empaths exhibit the globe through their intuition. Each Empath experiences overwhelm at some point, it's one among the foremost difficult aspects of being sensitive.

The overwhelm endured, from seizing an excessive amount of emotional energy from others can, at times, be unbearable. It's typically caused by being "peopled".

But being around crowded places or too negative folks is not the sole way.

An Empath becomes overwhelmed when somebody has caused them hurt, by their words or actions, or if they had negative thoughts directed towards them, it typically throws the Empath off-balance, causing them nose-diving.

Empath surge-over influence individual in a very totally different manner, some to a bigger extent, less fascinating at varied section of life.

This often results to extreme fatigue, depression and mood swings, it can trigger thoughts that keep you awake at night, and dark emotions that flatten you.

The best thanks to combat the impact of overwhelm is to require action as shortly as you become responsive to it.

Seizing the energies of others is exhausting work, particularly once those emotions are of lower vibrations appreciate grief, anxiety, fear, and anger.

These energies produce stress inside the body that will, in time, exhaust the sympathetic and para-sympathetic system while not the host even realizing it, that is, till you cannot appear to stay your eyes.

If you discover yourself dragging physically, chances are high that you have got internalized an excessive amount of what surrounds you and it's time to declutter.

When an empath has taken on too significant a dose of lower vibration emotions, he or she's begin to mirror and embody these emotions, typically leading to bouts of depression.

In these cases, an empath might address self-medicating. Every empath has his or her own purpose of overwhelm and you may discover yours in time, if you have got not already.

When you are finding out on negative emotions, energy, or maybe physical distress from folks around you, you may become inundated or physically unwell.

Even an overload of positive feelings might exhaust you, therefore it's vital to require the time you wish to reset.

If you cannot escape overwhelming emotions and rest your senses, you have a lot of possible to experience burnout, which might have a negative impact on well-being.

Arguments and fights may cause more distress, since you are not solely managing your own feelings and reactions. You are also engrossing the emotions of the others involved. Caring deeply can create it exhausting to inform folks once you approach the purpose of overwhelm.

Nevertheless, it's important to hunt a robust stance. Empaths may also be more at risk of manipulation or venomous behaviors.

Your earnest need to assist folks in distress will leave you unaware of signs of toxicity.

Good self-care practices and healthy boundaries will facilitate insulate you, significantly from negative emotions and energy.

However the emotional "noise" of the globe can cause important distress once you lack the tools to manage it.

If you are troubled to manage overstimulation on your own, and it affects your quality of life or keeps you from relationships and different personal goals, an expert can assist you learn to develop boundaries and determine useful self-care.

Remember, your desires and emotions are even as necessary because you decide up in everybody around you.

Empaths do usually feel overpowered and discouraged, tie down by the emotions that they are continually molding. When you are feeling somebody else's passion, it is draining. Over time, it will cause emotional burnout.

Emotional burnout is once you feel exhausted along with your emotions.

While anyone can expertise it, empaths are particularly vulnerable to their ability to soak up emotions from others.

The general public solely traumatize their own emotions or the emotions of these nearest to them. Emotions can be hard.

There are people everywhere the globe who cannot process their own emotions, however most of them are empaths.

Empaths are thus in tune with emotions that they will be standing next to somebody they are not grasp and feel what they are feeling.

Empaths may feel deeper than others, which implies typically they will feel upset or pissed off about things. This is traditional and zip to be embarrassed.

Excess emotions, even smart ones, can bring forth stress for empaths. You will often feel powerless or at a loss of what to do. Sometimes, it can even be that you are trapped.

This can be completely different than feeling tired or the requirement to "recharge" feelings.

Life as an empath will feel overwhelming, however the happy Empath provides you tools to assist you navigate charged emotional territory.

For an empath, walking into a thronged space can feel overwhelming, talking to individual who is disquieted or angry is demanding.

Being ready can help to avoid sudden emotion overload. The trick is to notice down what triggers your empathetic tendencies, and having a thought for each.

Some of these can involve the boundary work, others will like a recovery plan, keeping the day when free of rest and self-care.

Having these plans can save tons of your time (and energy) once a state of affairs presents itself. Empaths all over are taking up more feelings than ever, and apace developing emotional overwhelm.

You enter a state of emotional overwhelm when the intensity of emotions you are feeling outweigh your ability to handle them.

When empaths are exposed to a lot of great negative emotions, they will be quickly powerless and notice themselves unable to control what they are experiencing.

In a state of emotional overwhelm, your ability to suppose and be rational is hindered attributable to the mess of thoughts in your mind.

This painful state of mind get within the manner of existence if it's not self-addressed well. It might even disrupt relationships if it prevents correct rationalization and communication.

It's common for non-empaths to experience emotional overwhelm too.

There are a full host of doable causes, resembling stress, trauma, tough relationships.

Major life changes or events, can bring forth emotional overwhelm for anybody.

This means empaths could be taking up multiple doses. In any situation, it's necessary to be able to observe once you are developing emotionally before it's too late.

Most notably, emotional overwhelm can cause a giant reaction to ostensibly tiny problems. Once your bucket is full, even the tiniest droplets will cause it to overflow.

When your mind is littered with too several thoughts, feelings, and emotions, as empaths usually are, you may have issue that specialize in tasks you are speculated to be and may even end up troubled to sleep, despite feeling a lot of tired.

Emotional overwhelm can be similar to depression. The inability to process negative thoughts means you might not feel the same joy during usually "good" experiences.

Emotional overwhelm, much like any mental health issue, can cause physical symptoms.

The tension in your body caused by being under inescapable stress can lead to headaches and muscle pains and even nausea and dizziness.

Ultimately, emotional overwhelm can resulted in cancelled meals, failed projects and end to relationships. Fortunately, emotional overwhelm does not have to be a long-term issue.

There's no need to let the emotional overwhelm take over your life. Handling emotions as an empath is almost second nature. The easiest way to cope with emotional overwhelm is to reduce the influx of negative stimuli.

Try to stay away from places online where people might be sharing their negative feelings. It might feel wrong at first, but any empath should also consider limiting their time as a friend's "shoulder to cry on".

Right now, everyone has very intense emotions and if it's not going to be healthy for you to take on multiple cases of distress, it might be best to be honest and admit you cannot be their go-to for now.

When you feel the negative effects of emotional overwhelm coming on, try bringing your attention back to your body instead of your mind. You could try fidget device for a momentary distraction.

Exercise of any form is a great physical distraction. The inexperienced empath is usually overwhelmed by the sudden flood of information received. Feeling overwhelmed on an on-going basis probably means that you are a highly sensitive Empath.

When we feel overwhelm for any length of time our bodies begin to struggle with that overloaded feeling and the energy gets lodged in various parts of the body connected to the nervous systems. Over time this can build up health problems develop such as; Chronic Fatigue and Headaches.

EMPATHY FOR ANXIETY IN RELATIONSHIPS

Empathy — the ability to tune into and share another person's emotion from their perspective plays a crucial role in bringing people together.

It is an essential ingredient for building intimacy in relationships.

With emotional empathy, you actually put yourself in someone else's shoes and feel their emotion and then there's compassionate empathy, where we feel concern about another's suffering, but from more of a distance and with a desire to help the person in need.

The perspective we take when responding to someone else's suffering can affect our own health and well-being.

A person who is avoidant of close intimacy may experience cold, emotionally unavailable, without empathy, or even stand-offish, even though they may long for.

While anxiety can be healthy, it can motivate people and/or help them sense danger within their environment, for people with GAD, their anxiety is overwhelming and debilitating, which can be extremely detrimental to relationships.

One way to keep empathy in check is through compassionate contemplation.

Transforming initial emotional empathy into compassion does not mean you care less about the person.

We learn to control and handle our empathy, as we do other emotions, and even change excessive emotional empathy into less stressful compassion.

Emotional empathy can cause pain and burnout, compassion drives you to want to help. Living with anxiety can be tough — your thoughts might race, you might dread tasks others find simple (like driving to work) and your worries might feel inescapable.

But loving someone with anxiety can be hard too. We feel powerless to help or overwhelmed by how our partner's feelings affect our daily life.

We often find that our partners are somehow intertwined in their anxiety.

Anxiety is experienced at many different levels and in different forms from moderate to debilitating, from generalized anxiety to phobias and its impacts can vary.

Anxiety does not have an easy solution, but helping someone starts with compassion. When partner suffers from debilitating anxiety, their behavior can be frustrating, in other words, encouraged partner to overcome their anxiety and do not let partner's anxiety run family's.

A lot of people with anxiety disorders understandably view anxiety as the enemy, actually, it is not.

The real enemy is avoidance; it reduces the number of life experiences shared by partners.

Anxiety causes period of panic, feelings of fear or overwhelm, and a general sense of unease and tension. It takes over thoughts and bleed into several areas of life.

If you are feeling a strain on your relationship, anxiety is also enjoying a role. Anxiety causes concern or worry which build us less tuned in to our true needs in an exceedingly given moment.

It also can make us less attuned to the requirements of our partner. If we tend to be troubled concerning what can be happening, it's tough to concentrate to what's happening.

When we feel overwhelmed, our partner may feel as if we are not present.

If you notice a concern that causes your thoughts to stray from the facts or this moment, pause and rely on what you recognize (as opposition what you do not know).

Relax before you build purposeful steps to make trust in our partner.

Share overtly once we are feeling worried, and consciously reach set our partner (physically or verbally) when we would possibly unremarkably withdraw or attack in fear.

Someone who tends to agonize may have trouble expressing his or her true feelings.

It conjointly also tough to keep affordable boundaries by posing for the eye or area that's needed. Since encountering anxiety is unbearable, subconsciously we tend to try and adjourn the experience of it.

On the opposite hand, worry will cause us to believe that one thing should be talked concerning immediately, once after all a brief break is also observed.

If we do not specify what we actually feel or need, anxiety becomes stronger.

Plus, our emotions might eventually spiral out of control if we keep them in, we became weak and defensive.

Our worries and fears puts excess pressure on our relationship, we desire to like stress so as to guard ourselves in relationship, however it would be keeping us from being compassionate and vulnerable with our lives.

If your partner experiences anxiety, you will build up rancor and react in self-serving ways as we tend to toll. The attitudes and views that we have got are contagious.

Keeping our stress levels beneath permanent control is actually laborious once our relation is feeling worried, upset, or defensive. After you notice yourself turning into fearful or defensive, take a flash to think about the compassion that you simply have for yourself and your partner.

Clearly ask for the support you wish to feel white-haired and understood. Apologizing for lease anxiety cause self-absorbed. Experiencing joy is a way of safety or freedom. Anxiety makes us feel either fearful or limited.

Negative thoughts and fears impact a person's ability to be gift at intervals in a relationship, probably intake the thrill out of a moment bearing in mind to laugh and play along with your partner.

Joy physically heals and comforts your brain in ways which are important for a healthy relationship. Building trust within your relationship could scale back the faculty of anxiety. By understanding however anxiety impacts your relationships, you will be able to produce positive modification within a relationship dynamic.

Building trust within relationship reduce the power of anxiety. By understanding how anxiety impacts relationships, we have a tendency to create positive change within a relationship dynamic.

A loved one can do everything they can to assist their relative overcome anxiety. Anxiety causes plenty of strain on relationships which can become terribly isolating.

There are many various degrees of anxiety and each can have an effect on relationships differently. Anxiety impact relationships in a variety of various ways that depends on the symptoms that are experiencing.

For some, it would cause them to become excessively keen about their lovers whereas others might isolate themselves for worry of embarrassment or changing into a burden.

Sometimes anxiety can cause an individual to become overly dependent, their anxiety might make them nervous to be alone or to face bound things on their own.

Anxiety additionally cause an individual to question each call they build, which might also lead overdependence. Due to this, somebody with anxiety may need a relentless want for closeness to their friends, family, or partner, and crave constant support from them.

This overdependence cause overthinking around social interactions, leading them to worry once someone does not respond quickly via phone or social media.

People who are excessively keen about their relationships may struggle with effective communication and assault in ways in which are harmful to their relationships.

People with anxiety isolate themselves and become avoidant of relationships to avoid negative feelings (like being discomfited by or frustrated with an admirer.

It will be troublesome to open up and be vulnerable with those you are nearest to as others would possibly understand you as cold, stand-offish, or showing emotion unavailable although long produces maintaining and making new relationships very difficult, and generally impossible.

Anxiety is not a straightforward factor to overcome and it should even be one thing you upset throughout life. However, there are still ways that to keep up and nurture relationships despite stricken by anxiety.

To enhance sympathy towards partner, first, it's important to explore "what's entering into manner of its natural expression.

A giant obstacle in feeling empathy toward our partners is obtaining entangled in our own perspective and therefore the intensity of feelings.

When we have a tendency to listening with real attention, we are taking action to know our partner. Having empathy for others is vital all through relationships.

We demonstrate our empathetic talents for a partner by characteristic what that person is feeling. To possess empathy for different individuals, we have a tendency to be in reality with our own feelings.

Great listening talents are valuable to modify good communication between partners. The single most significant relationship skill required is sympathy — the power to know and share the sentiments of another.

Sympathy is the heart of a relationship and without it, couples cannot bond and connect to at least one another properly. Human beings are wired to bond.

Sympathetic people see the innocence in others, instead of judging them. Human personalities are very complicated and unique.

Everyone has their own safety desires in relationships. By asking questions and listening, we have a tendency to discover partner feelings showing emotion safe.

Empathy may be a necessary precursor to intimacy, trust, and belonging. It's the sensation that produces it troublesome to show a blind eye to the suffering of others.

Empathic individuals bear variety of happy moments. Sympathy typically strengthen selfless behavior, and empathy-based kindness has been shown to prolong cooperation and forgiveness, strengthen relationships, scale back aggression and judgment, and even improve and strengthen mental and physical.

Practicing the key parts of empathy will facilitate higher perception and move with people in life. Sympathy begins once the intention of listening for feeling is set.

Making a shot to notice the signals individuals are giving will indicate what they are feeling. Emotions create a big barrier when it involves noticing what others are feeling.

Making an effort to actively listen facilitate and strengthen emotional understanding and sympathy.

Once emotion is acknowledge in another person, empathy puts you squarely in this person's shoes. Empathy is not feeling what you would feel in that situation; it's stepping beside and adopting emotions for a number of moments.

After we see our partner going through a tough time, make sure to pay attention and share, however clearly determine what will be done to be of help.

The follow-through on sympathy means that initiating positive modification for others. The gorgeous factor regarding empathy is that once others begin to flourish, it improves our own life as well.

Empathy is very important in almost each facet of daily life. It permits a nation to own compassion for others, relate to friends, idolized ones, co-workers, and strangers, and it's an outsized profit impact on the world. Healthy relationships need nurture, care, and understanding.

A friendly relationship or romantic relationship that lacks fellow feeling and understanding can presently flounder. When folks solely consider their own interests, the opposite people within the relationships will suffer. Each people in a relationship bring their own ideas, life experiences, and struggles.

Without taking the time to relate to another's feelings and perspectives, people in relationships likely feel unloved and uncared for.

When we take the time to listen to the things that other people are telling us, it is an easy way of understanding how they think and feel.

Listening is best achieved when we set aside our own thoughts and opinions and carefully think about what another person is saying. To expand empathy, a person might have to challenge pre-conceived notions and biases and consider another person's point of view.

One of the qualities of effective communication is the use of empathy. Communication is very important in relationships because it permits partners to share their interest, concerns, support every other; organize their lives and create decisions; and it allows people to related well.

Effective communication is predicated on the approach that we tend to speak and listen, and the way we respond and our body language. Fellow feeling helps a nation perceive the good truth of relationships.

When we are ready to change another person's shoes and see life from their own view, situation, belief and struggle, we are then higher equipped to connect, while not reactivity.

It is, in a very way, a symptom of generosity; not within the material sense, however rather it's a spirit of generosity. By leaning into this generosity and learning a way to be a lot of empathetic, we cultivate a perspective of openness, and that we train our minds to be marveled.

Fellow feeling completely impact our relationships, with ourselves and others. Empathy has multiple components: the cognitive, wherever we understand the person's thoughts or feelings; the emotional, where we will share these feelings; and therefore the compassionate, where we transcend sharing concern and actively try and cut back someone's pain.

Someone with anxiety can react to relationship stress with a fight-or-flight response, as if the strain were a physical attack.

Generally, upset thoughts do encourage partners to act in ways in which trouble out and strain their relationship. Nonetheless, anxiety does not have to break relationship or place a strain on the purpose wherever it's exhausting to enjoy.

By understanding anxiety generally and the way it affects each partner and relationship, we will love one another deeply and connect in a very new way.

Educating yourself also can relieve tons of the strain. Individuals with anxiety problems or an anxiety disorder, however, tend to own these anxious thoughts often and more intensely. Anxiety does not have to place relationship in jeopardy.

By mistreatment the proper strategies, we will have a healthy relationship and stop anxiety from inflicting an excessive amount of stress.

Nonetheless, one of the foremost effective ways to traumatize anxiety in a relationship is to speak concerning it openly, honestly and directly with partner.

Anxiety causes stress as a result of what we tend to instinctively understand as a problem, nothing of much significant. This evokes association and concern. Anxiety is not solely a supply of stress in a relationship. It's additionally a chance to grasp and love your partner more deeply.
Worry is an active fear response, individual experience, it should now and then focus on excessive amount on his or her own considerations or challenges.

Worries and fears is also golf shot inessential pressure on relationship. If partner experiences anxiety, it builds up bitterness and react in inconsiderate ways as well.

Anxiety feels flighty and there's typically nothing that feels higher than having somebody beside you who's grounded, out there and okay to travel through this with you while not attempting to alter you.

Every relationship comes with its share of challenges. There are also times once your partner is swamped by anxiety, they act in a very method that appears irrational to you (crying, yelling, talking in circles).

However, to abstain from creating true worse, keep yourself quiet. Pointing out common erratic behavior is not aiming to facilitate them resolved or act rational—it can solely create things worse, and cause them to continue.

Instead, take a deep breath, remember that your partner is in pain, and stay calm. Validate how they are feeling and listen to what's going on. Everyone is susceptible to day-to-day stress manifesting as worry about a relationship, fear of the dating process, or trouble communicating with a partner.

People who feel unsteady in a relationship may be tempted to avoid or distract from the issues causing problems. Avoiding is only a temporary solution, and it often ends in heated conflict. Set a standard for addressing issues head on in the relationship, even if it feels uncomfortable at first.

EMOTIONAL INTELLIGENCE AND SELF ESTEEM

Emotional intelligence is the ability to grasp and manage own emotions and the people around you. People with a high degree of emotional intelligence know what they are feeling, what their emotions mean, and the way these emotions will have an effect.

It is vital to own a solid understanding of how our emotions and actions affect the people around us. Emotions intelligence helps to alleviate stress, communicate effectively, sympathize with others, overcome challenges and remove conflict.

Fellow feeling will increase life satisfaction, emotional intelligence and self-esteem.

People with high empathy have larger and a lot of fulfilling social networks, a lot of social lives, volunteer more readily, give more to charity and are more possible to assist others.

Emotional intelligence helps build stronger relationships, accomplish career and private goals. It also can assist you to attach along with your feelings, turn intention into action, and make knowing choices regarding what matters most.

Uncontrolled emotions and stress can also impact mental health, making you liable to anxiety and depression. Inability to understand, get comfy with, or manage emotions result in struggle to make strong relationships.

This successively may end up into feeling lonely and isolated and additional exacerbate mental state problems.

By perceiving emotions and the way to regulate them, we tend to be ready to specify how we feel and understand how others are feeling.

This permits us to speak more effectively and forge stronger relationships, each at work and in personal life. Being in tune with our emotions serves a social purpose, connecting us to people and also the world around us.

Social intelligence enables us to acknowledge friend from foe, live another person's interest in us, cut back stress, balance our nervous system through social communication, and feel worshipped and happy.

Emotions are necessary items of knowledge that tell you things regarding yourself and others, however within the face of stress takes us out of our comfort zone, we are able to become swamped and loosen.

With the flexibility to manage stress and keep showing emotion present, we tend to learn to receive disconcerting information while not letting it override our prosperous leads which ought to savvy to sympathize with others, if you wish to earn their respect.

Most individuals feel many alternative emotions throughout the day. Some feelings (like surprise) last simply a few seconds. Others could keep longer, making a mood like happiness or sadness.

Being ready to notice and accurately label these everyday feelings is the most elementary of all the emotional intelligence skills.

Being attentive to emotions and easily noticing them as we tend to feel them helps us manage our own emotions. It conjointly helps us understand how people feel.

However, some people might undergo the whole day while not extremely noticing their emotions, create it a daily habit to bear in mind your emotions. Individuals are naturally designed to grasp others.

Part of emotional intelligence is having the ability to imagine how people may feel in sure situations.

It's regarding understanding why they feel the way they do. Being ready to imagine what someone emotions is probably to be feeling (even once you do not truly know) what is named empathy.

Fellow feeling helps us care about others and build sensible friendships and relationships. It guides us on what to mention and the way to behave around somebody who is feeling sturdy emotions.

Someone who possesses good emotional intelligence is aware of that it will harm relationships, to resist emotions in a very means that's too strict, too impelling.

Part of managing emotions is selecting our moods. Moods are emotional states that last a bit.

We have the facility to make your mind up on what mood is for a situation, so as to urge into that mood. Choosing the proper mood will facilitate somebody get motivated, target a task, or strive once more rather than giving up. Individuals with sensible emotional intelligence grasp that moods are not simply things that happen to us.

We can manage them by knowing that mood is best for a selected state of affairs and the way to urge into that mood.

We are able to work to create even stronger emotional intelligence skills simply by recognizing what we feel, understanding how we got there, understanding how others feel and why, and golf our emotions into earnest words once we needed.

It's clear that we are all showing emotional intelligent however we would like to require longer to self-assess and work on our emotions. The talents concerned in emotional intelligence are self-awareness, self-regulation, motivation, empathy, and social skills.

There could be a time within the lifetime of each plight wherever it's ripe for resolution. Emotions offer the cue to act once a haul is sufficiently big to see, nonetheless still sufficiently small to solve.

By perceiving your emotions, you move adeptly through your current challenges and stop future ones. Emotional intelligence (EQ) is that "something" in every people that is small amount intangible. It affects how we have a tendency to manage behavior, navigate social complexities, and build personal choices that win positive results.

Emotional intelligence is the ability to acknowledge and understand emotions in ourselves and others, and skill to use this awareness to manage behavior and people who fail to use their emotional intelligence skills are seemingly to show to other, less effective suggests managing their mood.

They are doubly as likely to experience anxiety, depression, substance abuse, and even thoughts of suicide. Emotional intelligence includes a sturdy influence on health-related outcomes as a result of reducing the perception of stress in response to attempting situations.

Emotional intelligence skills strengthen brain's ability to deal with emotional distress. This resilience keeps system strong and protection from disease.

Emotional Intelligence, and our ability to draw on as a reserve helps us in such a lot of ways: from helping in taking care of our physical and psychological state and well-being, through our ability to inspire and lead. It's our ability to manage effective relationships. Fellow feeling is not regarding being heat and fuzzy, however about the flexibility to speak that just will see the world from another's side of view.

It includes a psychological feature dimension (understanding the tasks an individual should perform) and an emotional dimension (acknowledging the humanity of another person before coming into a dealings).

By sharing someone's experience, you identify ground and rapport to induce things done together. Emotional intelligence is the capability to acknowledge the impact our own feelings wear ourselves and to tune into the sentiments of these around us, to manage our emotions and our actions, and to move skillfully with the individuals.

Those who lead with Emotional Intelligence are highly equipped to inspire and mobilize others towards creating a positive impact within the world. Empaths develop sturdy emotional connections to others and skill higher levels of sensitivity to their surroundings.

As a result, several people with this temperament kind need time on their own to decompress and center their focus and attention. Empaths are sensitive individuals, who have a keen ability to sense what individuals around them are thinking and feeling. While some people have a tough time deciding what those around them are feeling, empaths usually grasp directly how alternatives feel. Some empaths often realize themselves fully by the emotions of others, however other empaths have found ways to separate their emotions from those they sense, creating their fellow feeling a quality to operating with giant teams instead of people who decide themselves.

Empaths feel emotions a lot and intensely than the individuals around them. It's additionally potential that they are having problem processing social situations, as not all people with high emotional intelligence feel full once confronted with the emotions of others.

What some establish as empathy may be hypersensitivity. As an empath, it will typically be terribly confusing when people act during a bound way, the very fact that we have a tendency to feel things deeply while not even a word spoken can then leave our mind to run completely different thoughts, feelings, and emotions.

The awareness that solid emotional intelligence will offer for somebody of an empathetic nature is second to none. It's the grounding that's necessary so as to gifts naturally and unapologetically, and by understanding the tapestry of human emotions and trigger points, we have a tendency rather more able to pick out and improve or boost decisions.

Sometimes as an empath, you are left confused by the manner individuals behave, you are left utterly drained of your energy, and while strong boundaries are key in sure situations, there may be very little doubt that a heightened awareness around emotional intelligence will alter you to not solely.

Emotional intelligence makes us additional driven and action-oriented. Individuals with a high emotional intelligence perceive work-place dynamics and are capable of being a team player. People with strong emotional intelligence will solve drawback and handle stress well.

They gain leadership roles than to their social and conflict-resolution skills. Maximizing emotional intelligence develop a powerful and healthy outlook so on surpass all told areas of life with peace of mind and golf stroke.

Self-esteem are a few things Empaths struggle with on a daily, if not hourly basis.

Empaths are particularly vulnerable to low self-worth, rather to their extremely sensitive nature, Empaths take everything to heart. This may be a sensible quality, it's what helps to form an Empath. An Empath, however severally realize it arduous to manage such intense sensitivity, usually leading to low morale.

The inner storms that an Empath experience cause such an individual to feel confused and pissed off to the point of depression. Depression is incredibly abundant unmoving in low self-esteem, whereas developing a healthy self-esteem is a powerful tool in combating depression.

Self-esteem is sort of instantly improved once an individual involved notice that they are not crazy or mentally deficient. The trademark of an empath is feeling and riveting different individual's emotions and/or physical symptoms than to their high sensitivities.

These people filter the planet through their intuition and have a tough time intellectualizing their feelings. Although sympathy is taken into account as an important indicator for mental health, vanity may additionally be viewed as a sensitive indicator of mental health.

 Positive self-esteem is assumed to be a necessary prerequisite for a well-developed empathies ability. Empaths with low vanity can suffer rather more than those with healthy balanced self-esteem. Being an empath may be confusing, and it can be terribly straightforward responsible to the despair and worthlessness we feel on the bombardment of stimuli we experience each day.

Empaths have low self-esteem as a result focusing on an excessive amount of others. In doing so, they are do not understand who they are, they cannot illustrious what's their energy and what belongs to others.

Self-esteem is the opinion we have in ourselves. After we have healthy self-esteem, we tend to feel positive about ourselves and about life in general. It makes us better able to deal with life's ups and downs.

When our self-esteem is low, we tend to see ourselves and our life in a more negative and critical light. We also feel less able to take on the challenges that life throws at us. Living with low self-esteem can harm mental health and lead to problems such as depression and anxiety.

Some of the experiences of low self-esteem can be signs of a mental health problem, particularly if they last for an extended time or have an effect on our state of mind. Having a mental state drawback may cause us low vanity, and feel more durable to cope or take steps to enhance our self-esteem. People with high self-esteem usually feel sensible regarding themselves and their progress through life. Individuals with low self-esteem often feel shame and self-doubt.

They often pay legion time criticizing themselves. Low self-esteem may be a symptom of several mental health conditions. Several individual acknowledge the worth of raising our feelings of self-worth.

When our self-esteem is higher, we have a tendency to not solely feel higher regarding ourselves, we are additional resilient as well. Vanity is made by demonstrating real ability and accomplishment in areas of our lives that bear on us.

Unfortunately, once our self-esteem is low, we are doubtless to wreck it even more by being self-critical. If our emotions are not activated or recognized, then the feeling that our lives have real meaning is negated, creating us pissed off that others either cannot share our feelings or refuse to share them with us.

People with sensible intentions generally try and calm sensitive feelings, however they end up underestimating them. If you are an empath you are finely tuned to the pain of different individuals, tending to attribute it as your own. Remember that there's solely such a lot you genuinely do to assist other people. Of course, you can try and help them or guide them by maximum amount as you see fit, however at the tip of the day the person experiencing the first pain should be willing to help themselves for any true healing to occur.

Often our caring natures blind us to the actual fact that a lot of people do not want, or are not ready to be fastened as a result the content within the safety.

Part of the attractiveness of distinguishing as an empath is that it generally provides access of escape to us; a chance to pin the blame on others. Yes, we would take in the emotions of others sort of a sponge, however that does not mean that we have a tendency to exempt from creating, and deeply experiencing our own emotions.

It is only too straightforward to portray ourselves as victims in life, and far more durable to require responsibility for our own happiness.

Empathy is very much an intellectual and emotional experience combined, whereas being an empath is a kinesthetic, physical and emotional experience. Yes, you might be able to share the feelings of another, but that does not necessarily mean that you understand the other person on a level deeper than emotions. Realizing that being an empath does not equate empathy helped me to grow immensely as a person.

As an empath it is so important that you incorporate some consistent form of catharsis into your everyday routine to rid yourself of the stuffy energy you might be harboring.

Putting yourself in the shoes of another person by practicing and expressing empathy builds your humanity and allowing yourself to receive empathy when you need it, to open yourself to its healing powers builds your own self-worth.

This journey through life is all about progress, not perfection and we can all lighten the load on the heavier days by opening ourselves to this beautiful emotion.

THE MENTAL HEALTH OF EMPATH

Empaths are people that fight the emotions and moods of others as their own. They are available into the world with heightened senses, that are accumulated more by completely different challenges or traumas they seasoned in their lives.

Empaths inhabit the whole and extreme opposite facet of the spectrum from people who are egocentric, psycho, or psychopathic. Empaths are those that have developed survival mechanisms once facing difficult environments in their childhood that polishing off into their adulthood.

They lengthen themselves outwardly, usurping and empathizing with the sentiments of others, even their offender. Empaths tend to spot and fight the underlying emotions of the opposite person.

This mechanism is meant for the Empath to check themselves as not break away others. Empaths got to learn to require care of themselves and become awake to their own feelings initial — a plan which will appear fully strange however is important for his or her purpose, survival, and it is sometimes troublesome for Empaths who have not managed their talents to be in relationships.

Whether or not their wounds are mirroring in the injuries of their partner, Empaths are completely in-tune with their partners to such an intense degree, that it's as if they are of course, there's some way for Empaths to possess and maintain healthy relationships.

Once Empaths comes into balance with themselves, relationships with them are still intense, however one thing resembling Heaven. Empaths are caring, thoughtful, warm, attuned to things on the far side the physical, completely caressive and accepting, and non-judgmental.

They are beyond supportive, captivating, and yes, will sympathize with their partner like no other.

Being extraordinarily sensitive to feelings makes empaths caring, tender, and understanding of other people. While most of the world struggles to place themselves in others' shoes, empaths possess a real superpower, the power to simply see a person's perspective as a result of feeling their emotions as themselves.

Looking at the opposite way, true issues comes with being so empathetic. Empaths most times feel misinterpreted majorly as a results of their deep feelings. They may become engulfed easily as they juggle all the emotions they experience from themselves and others. Feeling your own emotions may be exhausting enough.

But as an empath who picks up what everybody around them is feeling, it can quickly become means too much. This includes sturdy emotions of any kind from deep unhappiness to excitement and joy.

Empaths got to fastidiously manage their emotions and observe heaps of self-care to avoid constant emotional fatigue and exhaustion. At identical time, not having the ability to shut off compassion for those around, you will be able to feel significant and leave you carrying a lot of burdens you will not have control over.

When you are the one that feels suffering over anyone around you, it's exhausting to not feel to blame for remedying it. Having healthy boundaries is very important for all of us, however if you are an empath it may be significantly useful. Empaths often feel packed with different people's emotions that they lose track of their own needs.

Learning to mention 'no', knowing once to step far from situations, and prioritising self-care, is key. Deep sympathy provides us a special strength in relating and connecting to others. When we have a tendency to genuinely care, we are more apt to be ready to perceive another person in a means not each individual will.

Our sincerity can facilitate us to develop meaningful, fulfilling relationships. Relationships offer us an opportunity to not solely grow a deep sense of reference to another human being, however conjointly a chance to find out those that are integral to the human experience.

Recognition of empath tendencies may be a sensible thing. Empaths are an excellent resource for people. They listen well and supply great advice after they return from a healing space, they provide great companionship. As empaths in an unhealthy space, they may react to circumstances, numb out painful experiences, or become lost within relationships.

Many of us forget that we all possess one of the most effective tools to aid someone experiencing a mental health crisis. Empathy gives room to agree with other person or see things from the same point of view of others, which requires taking a moment to step outside of our normal patterns of thinking and feeling to imagine what it feels like to be the person in front of us.

The first way to diffuse a tense situation is to establish mutual relationship with the person in pain. Listening solemnly, without engrossing in problem-solving, signs that you are on that person's side.

All empaths are highly sensitive people, but not all empaths are alike. As an empath you may have traits of one or several different empath types and no matter what type of empath you are, you may frequently feel exhausted or debilitated due to taking on the pain of others.

There are many degrees of empathy and as an empath, it's likely that you reach different degrees of empathy during different times of your life.

That said, most empaths exhibit super traits. These include agreeableness, feeling optimistic about human nature, a willingness to compromise, and concern for social harmony.

In addition, most empaths are very trusting, and feel strongly invested in relationships.

Yet, for many empaths, no matter how hard you try to take care of yourself, you still end up sick, exhausted and with a slew of health issues you cannot understand.

The good news is, you do not have to sacrifice your well-being if you are an empath. There are ways you can take advantage of your innate strengths and goodness and you do not have to do anything extraordinary.

As an empath, everything you do to heal yourself actually helps to heal the planet, your mere presence on this planet is what creates the highest level of transformation for humankind.

BUILDING MENTAL HEALTH

Mental health is the level of psychological well-being or an absence of mental illness. It is the state of someone who is "functioning at a satisfactory level of emotional and behavioral adjustment. Mental health includes our emotional, psychological, and social well-being.

It affects how we think, feel, and act. It also helps determine how we handle stress, relate to others, and make choices.

Mental health is important at every stage of life, from childhood and adolescence through adulthood. Over the course of your life, if you experience mental health problems, your thinking, mood, and behavior could be affected.

Positive psychological state permits individual to comprehend their full potential, upset the stresses of life, work fruitfully and build significant contributions. Mental health refers to cognitive, behavioral, and emotional well-being.

Psychological state affects daily living, relationships, and physical health. However, this additionally works within the different direction. Factors in people's lives, social connections, and physical factors can all contribute to mental health disruptions. Taking care of mental health can preserve a person's ability to get pleasure from life.

Doing this involves reaching a balance between life activities, responsibilities, and efforts to achieve psychological resilience.

Conditions equivalent to stress, depression, and anxiety will all have an effect on psychological state and disrupt a person's routine.

Psychological state is "more than simply the absence of mental disorders or disabilities." Highest degree of mental health is concerning not solely avoiding active conditions, however additionally taking care of current well-being and happiness.

Protective and restoring mental health is crucial on a private basis. Everyone has some risk of developing a mental health disorder, irrespective of their age, sex, income, or ethnicity.

An outsized proportion of individuals with a mental health disorder have quite one condition at a time. It is very important to notice that psychological state depends on a fragile balance of things in many parts of life and also the world at large will work along to contribute. Mental health conditions equivalent to stress, depression, and anxiety which might develop because of underlying life-changing and physical health problems such as cancer, diabetes.

Anxiety disorders are the foremost common variety of mental illness, individuals with these conditions have severe concern for anxiety, that relates to bound objects.

Most people with an anxiety disorder try and avoid exposure no matter what triggers their anxiety. Post-Traumatic Stress Disorder occur once an individual experiences or witnesses a deeply disagreeable or traumatic event.

During this kind of event, the person thinks that their life or different people's lives are in danger. They feel afraid or that they need no control over what's happening. These sensations of trauma and concern may then contribute to PTSD.

Individuals may additionally see mood disorders as affectional disorders or psychical malfunction.

There is notable transformation in calmness of people with these state of being, typically neither insanity, characterized by a particular amount of depletion. Your psychological state influences how you think, feel, and behave in daily life. It additionally affects your ability to manage stress, overcome challenges, build relationships, and live through life's setbacks and hardships.

Strong mental health is not simply the absence of mental health problems. Being mentally or showing emotion healthy is far quite being freed from depression, anxiety or different psychological issues.

Rather than the absence of mental illness, mental health refers to the presence of negative characteristics. Having solid psychological state does not mean that you just undergo unhealthy moment or experiences emotional problems.

We all go through disappointments, loss, and pain and these are traditional components of life, they still cause sadness, anxiety, and stress.

However even as physically healthy individual are better ready to make a comeback from ill health or injury, people with sturdy mental health are better able to bounce back from adversity, trauma etc, this ability is termed resilience.

Those that are showing emotion and mentally resilient have the tools for handling troublesome things and maintaining a positive outlook. They stay focused, flexible, productive, in unhealthy times similarly as good. Their resilience also makes them less fearful of new experiences or an unsure future.

Even once they do not forth with knowledge, a retardant can get resolved, they are hopeful that an answer will eventually be found. Whether or not you are willing to alter a particular mental state problem, handle your emotions better, or just to feel positive and energetic, there are many ways in which to require control of your mental health.

Anyone can suffer from mental or emotional health issues and over a period of time most people will. Yet, despite how common mental health problems are, many of us create no effort to boost our situation.

We ignore the emotional messages that tell us what thing is wrong and check out confusing or influencing ourselves with drinks, medication and all.

We are thus engrossed with our challenges with the believe that people or our counterpart would not notice, we tend to hope that our scenario can eventually improve on its own or we merely provide up, telling ourselves this is often "just the approach".

The excellent news is you are not ought to feel bad. There are practices you will adopt to elevate your mood, become resilient, and revel in life more but even as it needs effort to make and maintain physical health, thus it's with mental health. We ought to work tougher to confirm sturdy mental health, just because there are such a lot of ways in which life takes a toll on our emotional well-being.

Many individuals think that if they are asked to facilitate for mental and emotional problems, the sole treatment choices offered are medication (which comes with unwanted facet effects) or medical care (which is long).

The truth is that, no matter your issues, there are steps you will be able to go to improve the approach you are feeling and bigger mental strategy. No matter what quantity time you devote up your mental and emotional health, you will still want the corporate of others to feel and performance at your best. Humans are social creatures with emotional desires for relationships and positive connections to others.

We seem to be meant to survive, including thrive, in isolation. Psychological feature perception yearn relationship despite the believe that the knowledge gathered create us lose hope of others.

The keys to move with somebody who may be a "good listener", someone you will be able to frequently discuss with in person, who will hear you while not their own conceptions of how you must. A good listener will listen to the sentiments behind your words, and would not interrupt, judge, or criticize you.

Reaching out is not a signal of weakness and it will not cause you a burden to others. Staying active is pretty much as good for the brain because it is for the body, the mind and also the body as such linked.

When you improve physical health, you will mechanically experience bigger mental and emotional well-being. Physical activity additionally releases endorphins, powerful chemicals that carry your mood and supply intercalary energy.

Regular exercise or activity will have a serious impact on mental and emotional health problems, relieve stress, improve memory, and assist you to sleep better.

Find out how to relief your stress levels is a good check. Stress takes a significant toll on mental and emotional health, so it's important to keep it beneath control.

Whereas not all stressors is avoided, stress control methods can help you brings things into balance. Face-to-face social interaction with somebody who cares concerning you is the only thing to calm your nervous system and relieve stress. It also releases stress-busting hormones, so you will feel higher though you are unable to change the nerve-wracking scenario itself.

Understanding and accepting your emotions particularly those unpleasant ones several people try and ignore can create an enormous distinction in your ability to manage stress and balance it up.

Everyone derives means and purpose in several ways which involve benefitting others, likewise as yourself. You may think it is some way to feel needed, feel sensible about yourself, a purpose that drives you on, or just a reason to urge out of bed within the morning.

In biological terms, finding means and purpose is crucial to brain health because it can generate new cells and build new neural pathways.

It may also reinforce your immune system, make hurt less severe, suppress pressure, and be centered to inspired the development of different actions towards enhancing our wellbeing and feelings.

We all generally get tired or overpowered by how we tend to feel or things do not stick to plan.

Having sensible mental state helps you lead a comparatively happy and healthy life. It helps you demonstrate resilience and also the ability to cope within the face of life's adversities. Sometimes, though the feeling or symptom is also yours and another person's.

Feelings are catchy, particularly if they relate to a hot button issue for you. Empath are susceptible to combat the emotional or physical pain that you simply have not puzzled out in yourself. The more you heal problems that trigger you, the less possible you will be to soak up emotions from others.

CONCLUSION

In conclusion an empath always puts people before themselves.

Empaths are giving, considerate and compassionate. We are broad minded, creative, problem solvers and thinkers. Often, we always search for answers because if there's a problem, there will be a solution and we will find one.

We love to research and educate ourselves. Empaths tend to not like any sort of modes that's negative or depressing as we take on those emotions too. Personally I do not watch TV or listen to the news at all. Music is all I need.

Empaths can go out of their way to help/satisfy the needs of complete strangers. Not because they want something in return. They do it to 'fix' things and to help people.

Empaths are great listeners. We absorb the emotions of people around us and we show great empathy when people are depressed. We feel their physical, mental and emotional pain.

We laugh when they laugh. Empath do not just sympathize what a person encounters, they put ourselves in the shoes of the person and feel what they feel like if someone is physically ill. But there are some people out there (eg narcissists), who identify and target empaths to feed their own egos and drain the good energy that empaths willingly give.

When empaths are around these people, we may feel exhausted a lot. We cannot fix these self-absorbed individuals. We need to acknowledge and accept some people cannot be helped and we need to learn to say no in order to keep our energy levels in a healthy state.

Crowded places may be overwhelming for Empaths as there is a varying degree of emotions all jumping out at you. We resonate the feelings and emotions around us. Empaths are also good at reading people. We mostly sit back and watch rather than be in amongst it all.

We love to have time to ourselves and often being outside in nature which reenergizes us. When our energy levels are low from people abusing what an empath is willing to give, the outdoors will help release those burdens.

Empaths feel emotions around them. Narcissists do not have real emotions. They mimic emotions of others. Then twist those emotions into negativity. Then they feed on the negativity.

This is detrimental for empaths. Empaths can find it difficult to distinguish their own emotions from the emotions of others. That is especially true when the emotion that the narcissists mimic started with the empath.

When the narcissist twists those emotions into something negative it will drain and exhaust the empath. This creates cognitive dissonance.

It takes time for an empath to heal. But once they do heal and learn more about themselves and the narcissism that causes them such detriment, they can learn to protect and strengthen their own natural abilities.

I believe that the narcissists targets empaths so aggressively in part because they are afraid of the strength of the empath who can turn it back onto them and shatter the narcissists image.

Made in the USA
Monee, IL
18 December 2021